Praise for Holy Hygge

I wasn't familiar with the word "hygge," but after reading Jamie Erickson's beautiful and thought-provoking new book, I won't easily forget it. Her refreshing honesty and real-life examples will inspire you to make your home and life a place for others to not only enjoy comfort and hospitality but so much more. Practicing *Holy Hygge* will let others know they are seen, known, and most importantly loved by a God who invites them to His table.

KATE BATTISTELLI
Author of *The God Dare* and *Growing Great Kids*

In the bleak midwinter, I sighed and told my kids we simply needed to "hygge harder!" But the crackly fire, cozy blankets, and hot tea didn't spark hope in our weary hearts. In *Holy Hygge*, Jamie Erikson explains *why* our efforts fell short: we needed Christ to warm us from the inside, to rest our souls, and to help us flourish in difficulty. I learned so much while reading this book: big ideas about the etymology of hygge and how it is a mere shadow of Christ's kingdom, and specific, practical ideas about how to commune with Christ, create a life-giving home, and welcome people in. Best of all is this: I've been looking for a book to read with my daughter before we launch her into the world next year. I want it to strengthen her understanding of Christ and the way He informs— and gladdens—the way we live at home and abroad. *Holy Hygge* is the book. If my daughter embraces the truths tucked inside, she'll be well on her way to living a good and satisfying life.

LAURA BOOZ
Author of *Expect Something Beautiful: Finding God's Good Gifts in Motherhood*

Holy Hygge will show you how to be the neighbor you wish you had and the neighbor the world desperately needs. It will help you rethink *home* and what it means to build a life that will leave an eternal legacy. It's a book to enjoy and share.

TRICIA GOYER
Bestselling author of eighty books, including *Heart Happy: Staying Centered in God's Love through Chaotic Circumstances*

Nestle your family into a peaceful haven of belonging and comfort. Jamie Erickson will show you how to establish and enjoy a home where Jesus is exalted, spirits are filled, and the best of life is lived.

GINGER HUBBARD
Bestselling author of *Don't Make Me Count to Three* and *Sam and the Sticky Situation: A Child's Book about Whining*; cohost of the *Parenting with Ginger Hubbard* podcast

In *Holy Hygge*, Jamie Erickson invites us into the cozy warmth of a home dedicated to God. Instead of settling for being just a place to lay your head, she offers practical ideas and inspiring practices that can transform our homes into a sanctuary, a place that can revive our communities and bring hope to a lonely and hurting world. Her story will give you the courage needed to create life-giving rhythms for yourself and your loved ones.

JENNIFER PEPITO
Author of *Mothering by the Book*

I had no idea what to expect when I started reading *Holy Hygge*. Immediately, I realized this was not a book to be rushed through, but savored. I found myself wiping away tears as Jamie explained this new concept to me. *Holy Hygge* is a gracious invitation for everyone who is weary and longing for home.

STACEY THACKER
Author of *Threadbare Prayer: Prayers for Hearts That Feel Hidden, Hurt, or Hopeless*

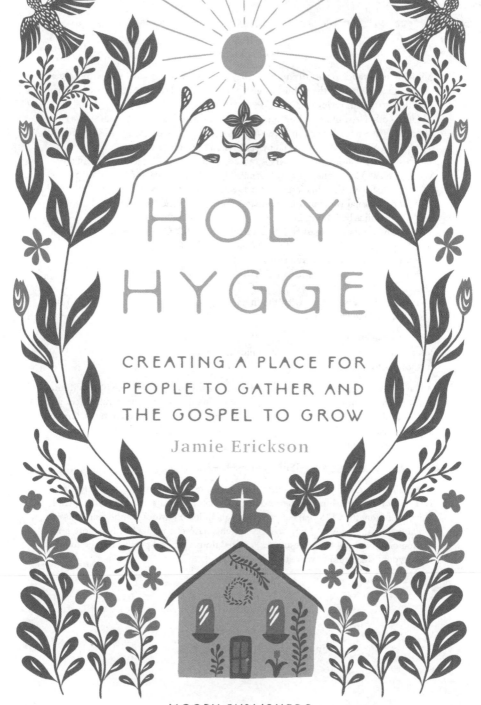

HOLY HYGGE

CREATING A PLACE FOR PEOPLE TO GATHER AND THE GOSPEL TO GROW

Jamie Erickson

MOODY PUBLISHERS
CHICAGO

Edited by Annette LaPlaca
Interior design, cover design, and cover illustration: Kaylee Dunn
Author photo: Dain Erickson

ISBN: 978-0-8024-2797-7

Originally delivered by fleets of horse-drawn wagons, the affordable paperbacks from D. L. Moody's publishing house resourced the church and served everyday people. Now, after more than 125 years of publishing and ministry, Moody Publishers' mission remains the same—even if our delivery systems have changed a bit. For more information on other books (and resources) created from a biblical perspective, go to www .moodypublishers.com or write to:

Moody Publishers
820 N. LaSalle Boulevard
Chicago, IL 60610

5 7 9 10 8 6 4

Printed in the United States of America

To Dain, my most favorite Dane

CONTENTS

MAKING HOME

If I find in myself a desire which no experience in this world can satisfy, the most probable explanation is that I was made for another world.

C. S. LEWIS

I'm pretty sure he'll be spending the entire day alone," the text read.

"What's his number?" I hastily tapped. "I'll have my husband give him a call and see if he'd like to join us."

With Thanksgiving only days away, a friend from church reached out on behalf of a recent widower in her neighborhood. With one of his daughters living across the country and the other spending a semester studying abroad, it seemed he'd most likely be eating his holiday meal at a local restaurant alone.

Having only ever talked with the man a few times, I knew an invitation to celebrate with my family would be a hard sell. We were practically strangers. I braced myself for a brush-off, mentally preparing bullet point rebuttals to any what-about-isms he might lob my way.

I don't know if it was his distaste for the mashed potatoes that would surely be served up with an ice cream scoop at the local diner or my promise to bake him a homemade apple pie that prompted him finally to accept our invitation, but he did. He arrived on our doorstep that blustery November night, the difficulty of the day etched across his entire face. After shrugging off his coat, he pushed a bouquet of wildflowers in my direction. "They were my wife's favorite. I probably should have put them in a vase," he mumbled. Briefly, the tension was palpable, but as all five of my kids scrambled toward him, hoping to be the first to show him the construction-paper placemats they had made, his features softened. His lips turned up slightly at the corners, and he let out an unfettered exhale, releasing weeks of loneliness and uncertainty. The rest of the night was spent in friendly conversation, enjoying stories of Thanksgivings past. Although at times he'd grow silent, with tears threatening to fall, he seemed relieved to know that all the parts of his life were welcome at our table, even the painful ones.

In truth, there was nothing remarkable about our time together. The meal was aggressively mediocre. The turkey was a bit dry, and the rolls were burnt on the bottom. But I knew he wasn't coming over to be fed. Not really. He was coming to belong. He was coming to feel at home again, if only for a few hours.

Though I had never experienced the death of a spouse, in my own small way I could relate to the sorrow that seemed to shadow this man's days. I was more than familiar with loss and could certainly empathize with the discomfort of wearing a life that didn't seem to fit. Home had often felt like a four-letter word to me too.

For my first twenty-two years, I lived in the inner city and surrounding suburbs of Phoenix, Arizona. Unlike most families I knew, mine moved from one apartment or rental home to the next, never living anywhere for more than twelve months at a time. Ours was a family of dysfunction, secrets, and addiction of every kind. Just when I began to settle into a neighborhood, discover the best bike routes to the nearest library, and learn the names of the kids next door, I'd stumble into a stack of cardboard boxes that my parents had lined against the living room walls, announcing yet another move. We were drifters with no real home.

I moved so often in my first two decades that I sometimes didn't even make the effort to unpack. A backpack was as good a spot as any to keep my favorite stuffed animal. Why search for thumbtacks to hang a poster when I would just have to tear it down in a few months? I longed to make *home*—a place constant and comforting, a place where I could make memories and put down roots.

Fast forward to my early adult years when I found myself married to my college sweetheart, a godly man of Danish and Norwegian heritage, whose growing-up years could not have been more different from my own. He woke up at the same address every morning for the first eighteen years of his life. His was a home of "sameness." His was the home I had always wished for. It was normal. At least that's what it seemed to me when I agreed to pack up all my worldly goods in Phoenix and follow him to Minnesota, the state that boasts the largest population of people of Scandinavian descent in the entire country. We set up house in a teensy apartment nestled in the woods. We were young, thirty pounds lighter, and quite naïve about what the next twenty or so years would look like. But we were in love, and this was our home. I was determined to make it a place where people wanted to be—a place where *I* wanted to be.

It didn't take long before *sameness* and *normalcy* lost their charm, though. This was *his* home. These were *his* friends. This was *his* family. Everything felt monochromatic and hollow. I was an outsider tagging along, struggling to be content with the sleepy pace of a one-horse town and losing the battle to stay warm in the near tundra where anything above zero degrees in January is considered a heatwave.

I cannot stress enough how fierce the elements are in Minnesota. For nine months out of the year, Minnesotans face freezing temperatures, biting winds, overcast days, and premature nightfall. It feels like the sun has all but forgotten this part of the world and refuses to shine for more than two seconds each day. It's bleak, to say the least.

Was this really what I had signed up for when I agreed to make a home in this state? I asked myself often. I felt lonely, cold, and misunderstood in this new place with these new people. I longed for home. Trouble was, I didn't really know where *home* was. I knew it wasn't *there*—moving from one ramshackle duplex to the next because my dad couldn't seem to hold down a job and keep up with rent. But it couldn't be *here*, where everything was different and yet always the same. Could it?

The culture and climate shock thrust me into an emotional tailspin. Little things began to fester and grow.

For goodness' sake, why can't Minnesotans call it a casserole *like everyone else in America? Why do they insist on calling it a "hot dish"?*

Duck, Duck, Gray Duck? Why are they teaching their children such blatant falsehoods? It's goose! *Duck, Duck, Goose!*

My teeth started chattering in September. It's now May. Should I see a dentist? I think my alignment might be off.

Everyone here seems so comfortable and cozy in the cold. Don't they know it's like −400 degrees outside? They're walking around in outfits so skimpy they could be folded up and shoved inside a sand-wich bag for easy travel. Meanwhile, I'm wearing every single sweater I own. I look like the Stay Puft Marshmallow Man.

Why can't I be happy like other women at work, at church, at the grocery store? Everywhere I go, everyone looks so content.

Why is it taking me so long to make real connections? I thought staying meant I'd make lasting friendships.

I know that I chose this life, but I thought things would be different. I thought things would be better.

Home is supposed to be the nicest word there is. Why do I always bristle when I say it?

Like the children of Israel who came upon the bitter, undrink-able water of Marah in Exodus 15:22–27, I went looking every-where for something to make life sweet—something to help me like living in Minnesota. That's when I began to look closely at those around me—to notice what made them so hearty and heartwarming. Despite grim and often uncompromising weather conditions, not to mention some very difficult life circumstances, my Scandinavian friends and family seemed unshakable. This was especially true for the ones who had put their hope and trust in Jesus. They were not only content; they were joyful.

The tenacity of spirit and strong resolve found in their homes wasn't just due to their thick skin, as some have jokingly suggested. It was more than that. The difference between them and me was that they had learned two simple truths that intersect at the core of their Danish way of life—a lifestyle I would learn to associate with the term *hygge* (pronounced HYOO-guh):

1. You can't always change your circumstances; you can only change your perspective.

2. Your outer life will always affect your inner life.

Like the log thrown into the water by Moses on the shores of Marah, these two foundations were what made Minnesota living so sweet. I had the same water, but without *hygge* it had a bitter taste.

A *HYGGE* PRIMER

Hygge is a funny word. It's not one that rolls off the tongue with ease. Even after tapping it out on a keyboard for what feels like four million months, I'm questioning whether my spell-check will hold up. The entire process of training my computer *not* to autocorrect it into *huge* or *haggle* takes herculean effort.

The term stems from a sixteenth-century Norwegian word *hugga*, which means to comfort, console, or encourage. It is loosely connected to our English word *hug*.[1] While the word or derivations of it have been around for hundreds of years, it wasn't until the late nineteenth and early twentieth centuries, when the Danish people experienced a social shift from elite living to more domestic family life, that *hygge* began to transform the Scandinavian home.[2]

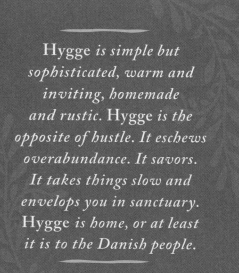

Hygge *is simple but sophisticated, warm and inviting, homemade and rustic.* Hygge *is the opposite of hustle. It eschews overabundance. It savors. It takes things slow and envelops you in sanctuary.* Hygge *is home, or at least it is to the Danish people.*

I wish I could scribble out a concise definition for you, one that wraps *hygge* up in a neat American package. But the truth is, *hygge* is hard to translate. There's no parallel English version. To complicate things further, it spans the Danish language, shrouding itself in several different parts of speech. *Hygge* is a noun. It's something you share, something that inspires you. *Hygge* is a verb. It's something you do either by yourself or with others. *Hygge* is an adjective. It describes peace, contentment, and joy. *Hygge* is a feeling, a concept, a lifestyle. In its most unsophisticated forms, *hygge* is a mindset—a way of making the mundane and necessary tasks of life more meaningful and beautiful.

When you sit in a comfy chair by the fire, that's *hygge*. When you arrange a fresh bouquet of favorite flowers on a bedside table, that's *hygge*. When you're sipping a frothy latte in an oversized mug, that's *hygge* too. Candles, soft furnishings, natural light, scents of nature, fresh-baked pastries, intimate gatherings with friends—these are all *hygge*.

Hygge is simple but sophisticated, warm and inviting, home-made and rustic. *Hygge* is the opposite of hustle. It eschews over-abundance. It savors. It takes things slow and envelops you in sanctuary. *Hygge* is home, or at least it is to the Danish people.

To be clear, the Danes don't hold a monopoly on comfy and cozy. Other Nordic and European cultures have put their own unique spin on *hyggelig* living (this adjective form is pronounced in Danish something like HYOO-guh-leh). In the Netherlands, it's *gezelligheid*. In Norway, *koselig*. *Lagom* is practiced in Sweden, while the Germans prefer *gemutlichkeit*.[3] All of these countries, while vastly different in customs and creeds, have found a common bond in their ability to build community, to invite closeness, to create well-being, and to celebrate the everyday.

Not surprisingly, this cultural liturgy has landed the Danish people in one of the top two spots of the European Commission's well-being and happiness index for the past forty years.[4] And why not? In a world largely defined by rush, *hygge* welcomes rest. It invites you to enjoy the simple pleasures of slow living, savored moments, and fostered friendships.

A TRENDING TOPIC

Hygge has become a cultural buzzword in recent years. One can't go far without stumbling into a bit of curated *cozy*, boxed up and shrink-wrapped for easy carry-out. *Hygge* has been mentioned on national commercials and garners an entire collection of home decor on Target.com. It was a runner-up for the 2016 Oxford Dictionary's word of the year,[5] was featured as the design aesthetic on HGTV's Urban Oasis 2019,[6] and has been hashtagged more than eight million times on Instagram.[7] It's a trending topic, to say the least.

Unfortunately, with popularity comes pollution. *Hygge* has been mismanaged and marketed in order to appeal to the masses. It's been relegated to store shelves, paint colors, and sound bites. In some ways, the commercialism of *hygge* has cheapened it. Most people don't truly even know what the word means or how to use it in a sentence. What's worse, the *hygge* frenzy has created a cult-like following of folks snatching up all the *cozy* they can in a relentless pursuit of happiness. Well-meaning women are buying fuzzy socks and flannel sheets, mugs, and bath salts. They're baking bread and drying flowers, throwing candlelit parties, and planning nature outings. They're sitting by fires and reading books with woolen blankets on their laps. *Hygge* has become the newest definition of health and well-being, a "healthy hedonism."

Of course, there's nothing wrong with pursuing coziness. But here's the cold hard truth: unless it's seen with a proper perspective, *hygge* will only ever be like fancy trim work laid over a shoddy foundation. To build a life-giving home, you need more than just essential oils and a high-priced entryway rug. Because the truth is, eventually the coffee will get spilled on the new chenille blanket and the cat will play tug-o-war with that favorite wool sweater. Someday the candle may tip, leaving you to watch the whole thing go up in flames.

Hygge is just a temporary fix. It's a lifestyle Band-Aid that will help create a home in the short term. True and lasting comfort, though, can't be tablescaped or found in some twelve-step Scandinavian formula. The perfect blend of coffee can't cultivate true contentment. There's no flannel blanket big enough to cover deep soul ache. A long walk in the woods won't change a life for the long haul. Reshaping an atmosphere can never permanently re-shape a heart. But it can help, especially when paired with the hope of Jesus.

JESUS AND

Please don't misunderstand me. I'm not suggesting that Jesus is somehow insufficient, that He falls short, or that He won't deliver on His promise to grant us all things that pertain to life (2 Peter 1:3). As a follower of Christ, I know the Lord can never be tacked onto something or made into an addendum to someone else's agenda. I give no merit to the "All I need is a little bit of coffee and a whole lot of Jesus" mantra. These types of sentiments might look great on the wall art and graphic tees pedaled online or at the corner gift shop, but they undersell the transforming power of Christ. We can't be glib about His finished work. We can't add or detract from it, making an idol fashioned to our liking. We don't need Jesus *and* fill-in-the-blank. All we need is Jesus. Full stop.

Perhaps it's that very sufficiency found only in Christ that makes *hygge* so compelling to so many. When you peel back the surface layers of this Scandinavian practice, you find seven tenets at its core. You don't have to look hard to see that they seem strikingly in line with the abundant life offered in Christ. Hospitality, thriving relationships, well-being, a welcoming atmosphere, comfort, contentment, and rest—these are the markers of *hygge*. But they're also qualities seen in the first Garden home and exhibited by Jesus.

When calculated with an earthly formula, these seven principles fall short and present a half-truth of what it means to build a sanctuary in this fallen world. A half-truth is just as dangerous as an outright lie, for it gives you a false sense of security, making you feel you've covered all your bases and checked all the boxes, when in reality, its bedrock is sinking sand.

Yet *hygge* can have a place in the life or home of a Christ follower. In the same way a favorite devotional book does not replace your time in God's Word but merely helps to set your gaze in the right direction and offer practical application to what you're learning in Scripture, *hygge* can be a kind of companion for making a home where people can feel their way toward God and find Him (Acts 17:27). When viewed correctly, *hygge* can be a physical tool that reflects your spiritual life and invites others into a relationship with Christ.

A NEW PROMISED LAND

One has only to look to the Old Testament to see how what is often viewed as a secular practice can have a sacred purpose. The Israelites of old were instructed by God to set up their home in the Promised Land in such a way as to show His holiness to the world. Their work and their rest, their daily rhythms and special rituals, their physical possessions or lack thereof, and even their very lives were to be a reflection of who God is and what He has done.

Twelve stones deliberately stacked just to the side of the raging Jordan River revealed the might of the hand of the Lord and how He had parted the waters on the people's behalf (Josh. 4:19–24). An annual seven-day stay in a thatched hut during Sukkot commemorated not just their deliverance out of Egypt, but also their Deliverer, the Lord their God (Lev. 23:42–43). Enjoying loaves of yeastless bread from the fifteenth through the twenty-first day of the first month became a lasting ordinance, to help the people remember how God passed over the houses of Israelites and spared their sons (Ex. 12:27). A small, ornate box hung on the side of each doorpost reminded the people of the ancient words of the Shema each time they entered and exited their homes (Deut. 6:4–9; 11:13–21).

Stones, huts, bread, and boxes— all these were outward displays of the inner life. They stood as both reminders and revelations of how the people of Israel were feeling their way toward and finding God. None of these practices added to their abundant life, the practices just recalled them to it and revealed their abundance to the world.

Our Land of Promise is no longer a place; it's a Person.

Stacked stones and thatched huts were for *then*—back when the Promised Land was a place. But now on the other side of the cross, the address has changed. Our Land of Promise is no longer a place; it's a Person. "I am the vine; you are the branches. Whoever abides in me and I in him, he it is that bears much fruit, for apart from me you can do nothing," Jesus said in John 15:5. That word *abide* means "to remain, to dwell."[8] It means to make *home*.

It seems natural to view *hygge* as something that belongs solely to the secular world. Perhaps that's because we're quick to divide our lives into two separate piles. The parts that pertain to God, His work, and our worship of Him are placed over *here*, and everything else gets put over *there*. We label certain kinds of music, certain kinds of movies, certain kinds of books as "Christian" or "sacred" and put all the rest in the "worldly" or "secular" category. But the truth is, in creating two separate columns, we forget that Jesus, our new Promised Land, was both fully God and fully man.

Jesus' life was not a dichotomy of sacred and secular. Every part had eternal weight. He was the Christ who just happened to be a carpenter. He spoke of the *someday* marriage supper of the Lamb but also celebrated the *here and now* wedding feast of a friend. He taught about living water and the bread of life but multiplied actual bread and fish for a hungry crowd. To suggest that some of His life was sacred and the rest was secular would be to deem only a portion of Christ's time here on earth to be "Christian." Jesus didn't split His life and time into spiritual and secular, and His outer life was exactly consistent with His inner life. He wisely recognized that outer behaviors affect and reflect the inner life.

> *For the believer there is nothing secular. It's all sacred when put under His authority for His kingdom purposes.*

He ably held on to both, and we'd do well to follow that example.

From the whispered prayers of Sunday morning to the late-night phone call to a friend on Monday night; from the altar we kneel beside in the church sanctuary to the sink of dirty dishes we lean over in the kitchen after supper, from the offering we drop into the plate as it passes down the pew to the 1040 form we submit to the IRS each April—every part of our lives has eternal weight. Since God is both Creator and Redeemer of all, and since, as 1 Corinthians 15:27 says, everything under creation is subject to Christ, for the believer there is nothing secular. It's all sacred when put under His authority for His kingdom purposes—and that includes the cultural practice of *hygge*.

CALLING ALL HOMEMAKERS

In complete transparency, I confess I'm not Danish. I'm not even a little bit Scandinavian. I didn't grow up in a *hyggelig* home. Truth be told, I wouldn't have even known what one was. Chances are, you're not Danish either. It doesn't matter. You're a woman created in the image of God and as such, you are a life-giver. You are a homemaker.

Homemaker. Now there's a word that has certainly fallen out of vogue in recent years. It feels old-fashioned and narrow-minded, restrictive even. But let's not forget that before God made humanity, He made a home for them. With breath-filled words, He hung the stars to drive the shadows away and flung the planets into motion, setting both time and space. Out of nothing, there was something. In the middle of it all, He built a sacred place, the first home. God was the first homemaker.

For Adam and Eve, Eden was the backdrop for building relationships, for nestling into a pleasant rhythm of work and rest, for finding comfort and contentment with God and with each other. *Home* in the Garden was perfect.

But as you probably know, sin came slinking in, covered in false hopes and empty promises and carrying an eviction notice. Because of God's holiness, a change of address was necessary. Adam and Eve had to somehow accept that their home was not their home anymore.

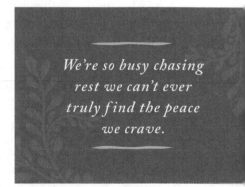

We're so busy chasing rest we can't ever truly find the peace we crave.

Sadly, ever since that grim day in the Garden when *good* was traded for *good enough*, all of humanity has been homeless. We're nomads, traveling this life doing our best to recreate that once-upon-a-time home. In our transient, mobile society, home often feels like a far cry from paradise. It's simply the place where our mail is delivered; a collection of rooms to store our stuff; a series of outlets for recharging our electronic lives. Even for those of us who never wander too far from our front stoop or dorm room door, home feels like a layover to the next big thing. We're lonely, anxious, overscheduled, and discontent. We're so busy chasing rest we can't ever truly find the peace we crave.

> *Your heart is Christ's home, and He's called you to lead others to that same Land of Promise.*

Our homes are anything but sanctuaries, and we secretly long for the life we see in those perfectly positioned nine squares over on Instagram—from the college graduate struggling to make a home completely from scratch to the single woman juggling the responsibility of making a home *and* a career, from the newlywed wrestling to combine *his* and *hers* in order to make a home that looks like *ours* to the mom straining under the weight of making a home that her children will both enjoy now and want to come back to someday. I don't know which of these women you are, but I know this: if you're a Christ follower, you're also a homemaker. Your heart is Christ's home, and He's called you to lead others to that same Land of Promise.

Hygge has been ingrained in the Danish people by the right of genealogy. It may not come as naturally to you, as an outsider. Unlike my friends and family, you've not been born cocooned in all its layers. Neither have I. But after two decades of living among folks practicing *hygge*, I've learned a few simple *hyggelige* habits to help me bring eternal sweetness to the world.

While in the center of a life of sameness, *hygge* taught me how to look for miracles in the mundane. When plagued with the perfection of Pinterest, *hygge's* simple aesthetic foundations helped me create a home atmosphere that reflected the beauty and comfort of Christ. Above all, when I was desperate to leave a legacy of faith, *hygge* showed me how to escape the pressure of a social media-saturated world and establish the kind of emotional, physical, and spiritual habits that can influence my friends, family, and neighbors for generations to come. It has helped me live a life of purpose on this side of the first Garden while I wait for my future home in the second. In the past twenty years, I've learned to be at home with *hygge*, and in turn, it has helped me be at home with *home*.

I share what I've learned from the place of a *student*, not as an *expert*. These chapters form a kind of CliffsNotes of my lessons learned. I've divided them into the seven tenets of *hygge* that seem to sync with the life of Christ. His life was more nuanced than what can be expressed on a seven-point list. But these seven categories represent the ways we can see *hygge* in Him, or more accurately, see Him in *hygge*. We'll look to the beginnings, in Eden, and show how *hyggelig* living mimics the perfection found in that first Garden home and later in the life of Christ. Then we'll explore the cultural applications of the Danish *hygge* lifestyle to look for simple and practical ways we outsiders can infuse them into our faith-filled homes in order to create a place for people to gather and the gospel to grow. The questions and Scripture readings included at the end of each chapter will help you consider *hyggelige* habits for making your *home*, and a brief prayer at the end of each chapter will draw you in closer communion with the One whose Spirit is making *home* in you.

The idea of *hygge* is compelling in our current culture of excess and isolation because it promises community, contentment, and rest. *Hygge* can cultivate all of those, but only when placed at the foot of the cross. The world is ripe for the comfort of real sanctuary living. The practices of *hygge*, in close cooperation with our trust in Jesus, can form a holistic approach to creating the kind of home and rich life that humanity has longed for since the perfection of the Garden.

HOSPITALITY

*When we sit at our tables, we're not just an aggregate of individual
family members eating and drinking to stay alive; we're a congregation
of communing souls hungering and thirsting to experience the goodness
and beauty of the life God has designed just for us.*

SALLY CLARKSON

Like any host excited to swing the doors wide to others,
God took great care when He created the Garden. He
prepared. He arranged. He readied. Thinking not just
of the needs but also of the unspoken and the not-yet-imagined
wants of those who would live there, He made a home. And it was
good. Not one item was out of place or unaccounted for. From
the swirling currents of the deep stirred by the raging wind, to the
tiniest blades of grass silently pushing their way up through a soft
cushion of fresh earth—His love was in every detail. When the
time was right, and when everything was ready, He invited others.

For Adam and Eve, Eden was not a home of their making. They were guests. But they cracked open the elaborate, garden-sized welcome basket of fruit and began to settle in. Hospitality began here—in the bushes. Home was good, but it was made *very* good simply because they were there (Gen. 1:31). It was a place where they could be seen and known and loved.

THE HOSPITALITY OF JESUS

Even after the fall and the displacement outside the Garden, the practice of hospitality remained. The descendants of those first two guests were charged to continue the open-door policy God demonstrated in that original home. Hospitality was not just a suggestion—a thing to do whenever they felt up to it—it was a command, given by God as a way to ensure that every outsider was welcomed. Leviticus 19:34 reads, "You shall treat the stranger who sojourns with you as the native among you, and you shall love him as yourself, for you were strangers in the land of Egypt: I am the LORD your God." In the same way that God had welcomed them—taken them as strangers in Egypt and given them a home—the children of Israel were to do that for others. The *love* mentioned here is *'āhab* in Hebrew. It is the same kind of love Scripture uses to describe the love a father has for his son and more remarkably, the love that God the Father has for humanity.[1]

Later in Deuteronomy 14:28–29, the Israelites were given more specific parameters for how to carry out this love, "At the end of every three years you shall bring out all the tithe of your produce in the same year and lay it up within your towns. And the Levite, because he has no portion or inheritance with you, and the sojourner, the fatherless, and the widow, who are within your towns, shall come and eat and be filled, that the Lord your God may bless you in all the work of your hands that you do." The plight of widows, orphans, and sojourners (foreigners or strangers, as some translations suggest) was bleak in ancient cultures. They lacked the familial or tribal status to provide for and protect themselves. This law was God's way of directly providing for the physical needs of the marginalized. In a broader sense, it foreshadowed the provision He would later extend to us, the church—foreigners of the faith, alienated from God.

Hospitality wasn't just important to the Israelites; it was a legal obligation. In accordance with the Talmud, *hakhnasat orchim* or the "bringing in of strangers" compelled Abraham to keep all four sides of his tent open in order that he would never miss a chance to invite others to his table.[2] It prompted Jethro to chastise his daughters for not inviting Moses in for refreshment. It encouraged the impoverished widow of Zarephath to provide a meal for Elijah even though her larder was empty. The law ensured that everyone was seen, known, and loved.

While the mandate of hospitality was written in ink, the blueprint for how best to welcome the stranger was sketched lightly in pencil. For the most part, God left the specifics up to the people. His only universal demand involved the same kind of hospitality He showed to His Garden guests: food. *Feed the stranger* was God's clear charge.

God called the Israelites to use the very thing that broke the relationship between Him and humanity in that first home—a bite of food—to help restore it. Food would reveal His *'āhaḇ*, His love, to the rest of the world. To share a meal with someone was to share life with them. It was a gesture of intimacy. It helped create a bond of unity between strangers in a way no other physical act could replicate.

As a Jew, Jesus would have been both giver and receiver of this same Levitical hospitality. The Son of Man came eating and drinking and invited others to do the same (Luke 7:34). All throughout the Gospels, we see Jesus building fellowship around a meal. At the table, He celebrated two becoming one, multiplied the faith and obedience of a small boy, extended friendship to the forgotten and the outcast, ushered in His greatest sacrifice, restored and promoted a three-time detractor, and comforted two weary travelers on their way home from witnessing the largest loss.[3]

> *As the Bread of Life, Jesus knew that inviting someone to the table was never just about eating. It was always about nourishment. It was always about life.*

Jesus bookended His ministry here on earth with meals, perhaps because He knew discipleship happens around a table. Vulnerability happens around a table. Accountability happens around a table. The table held so much potential that at one point when an offer of hospitality was not extended by a host, Jesus invited Himself. "And when Jesus came to the place, he looked up and said to him, 'Zacchaeus, hurry and come down, for I must stay at your house today'" (Luke 19:5). As the Bread of Life, Jesus knew that inviting someone to the table was never just about eating. It was always about nourishment. It was always about life—something Zacchaeus desperately needed, something we all desperately need.

In the final evening before His death, Jesus chose the familiarity of a Jewish feast to establish a new holy ordinance. His body would be broken. His blood would be poured out. The bread and the wine became tangible reminders of the communion the disciples would have with Christ and of the communion they'd eventually share with the whole congregation of believers that would come after Christ's death, hungering and thirsting for righteousness. That includes you and me (Matt. 5:6). The Lord's Table made us one in our need and freed us from the bondage of our sinful appetites.

Sometime later, when tasking Peter to build the church, the risen Jesus did not present a mission statement, a branding plan, or a five-point action initiative. He simply said, "Feed my sheep." In our modern attempt to dissect the seaside fish fry of John 21, we're often compelled to create a complicated formula for how Peter may have launched a "start-up" church from the ground level. "Preach to my sheep," "Equip my sheep," or even "Lead my sheep," never left Christ's lips. *Feed* was His rallying cry. Serve up generous portions of my *'āhab* to a world starving for "food that endures to eternal life" (John 6:27).

HYGGE HOSPITALITY

The Danish people know the power of hospitable living. Like Jesus, they've found practical ways to help people feel seen and known and loved. So much so that, unlike in America, where three out of five people confess to feeling lonely, Denmark boasts a surprisingly low rate of isolation and loneliness—only 3 percent according to the European Commission's most recent findings.[4] While that small figure can't all be credited to *hygge*, one could argue that the hospitality found at the very center of a *hyggelig* lifestyle prevents, or at least lessens, feelings of loneliness.

Strangers become friends around the table. That is why to the Danish people breaking bread together is one of the most *hyggelige* activities there is. Preferring to dine in rather than eat out, they don't just serve food at their tables, Danes serve meals. While every Danish table reflects the individual likes and dislikes of its host, they all have a few simple elements in common.

Candles. Light is a staple design aesthetic in every *hyggelig* home. Danes put candles everywhere, and the table is no exception. Candles elevate even the simplest meal and have a way of encouraging everyone to slow down and savor each bite.

Intimacy. While they occasionally host large parties, Danes prefer small circles of guests, no more than six at a time. The benefit of a small gathering is two-fold. First, small dinner parties require less planning, execution, and clean-up. A person is more likely to host several dinners throughout a month or season when the process can be kept small and simple. And second, smaller gatherings are naturally more intimate. When a group gets too large, the host is no longer building relationships and being hospitable; she's entertaining.

Potluck menus. Danish hospitality welcomes teamwork. At a *hyggelig* table, everyone has a role to play. Everyone is needed, and every contribution is valued. It's not uncommon for a host to ask a guest to bring something to contribute to the meal. In doing so, she's creating a familial atmosphere. A potluck lowers the expectations and welcomes imperfection. It makes the meal about the people gathered around the table and not the performance of those who prepared it. It ensures that guests with special dietary needs or preferences will be able to enjoy the meal too.

In America, potlucks are usually reserved for church basements or work break rooms. In Denmark, however, they're welcomed at every table. In fact, touted as their national dish, *smorrebrod* is a potluck on a platter. This unfussy, open-faced sandwich is made of dense rye bread topped with layers of this and that.[5] When served, guests are invited to bring whatever they have on hand that would create a unique "stone soup" kind of sandwich—from

sliced boiled eggs to leftover fish, from sauteed veggies to flavor-
ful cheeses. To the Danish people, a *smorrebrod* is a meal that says,
"I honor you and your needs and what you can contribute to the
communal table."

Rustic recipes. Because of their short growing season, Danish
food is simple. They eat what is available. Items are fresh, local,
and ethical. Their diet is largely defined by whole foods and rustic
comfort recipes centered on fish and various root vegetables. Some
might see a *hyggelig* menu as limited, but the Danish people prefer
to see it as a chance to create contentment around the table and
promote conscious consumption. Eating things in season means
you can't have everything you want when you want it. Instead, you
have to get creative and learn how to make beautiful use out of
what you have right now. It encourages healthy moderation and a
deep appreciation for those things that you can only enjoy every
once in a while.

Sippable drinks. Due to the frigid weather conditions known
throughout most of northern Europe, no *hyggelig* meal would be
complete without a warm mug of mulled cider, hot chocolate, or
coffee. Their drinks are slow, steamy, and sippable, inviting everyone to linger just a little bit longer around the table.

TABLE FELLOWSHIP

Hygge can help us create the kind of companionship and close community Christ was referring to when He called the disciples to feed
His sheep. The very word *companion* comes from the two Latin
words *cum* and *panis*. Together, they mean "with bread."[6] Could it
be Jesus knew relationships could grow and even be restored in the
span of time between bites? That strangers could become friends
when food was set between them?

> *The fellowship found around a table isn't like Grandma's fine china— reserved for only the important meals. It should be enjoyed in the ordinary moments of everyday life.*

Shared meals hold social and emotional power—from the complimentary cheesecake wheeled from the cafeteria to the hospital room of proud new parents, to the chicken salad sandwiches served up to a grieving family in the church basement, from the sizzling steaks ordered up to seal the deal over the lunch hour, to the tub of Ben and Jerry's finest brought over by a friend after a crushing breakup. From our first breath to our last, shared meals seem to always find a place in the big moments of our lives. The fellowship found around a table isn't like Grandma's fine china—reserved for only the important meals. It should be enjoyed in the ordinary moments of everyday life.

Yet our communal tables seem to be getting both smaller and faster. Studies show that nearly half of American adults eat most of their meals alone, and one out of five meals are eaten in a car.[7] Food has become a simple transaction. We're only willing to spend the time and social energy necessary to fuel our bodies. Relational interaction has become the exception and not the rule.

As followers of Christ, we need to do better. The nourishment we give and receive around the table is about more than just a plate of pasta or a bowl of beans. A meal around a table can potentially provide both an intentional place and an intentional time for people to build relationships through genuine conversations. By its very design, a table forces people into physical proximity, to sit, to slow down. Eyes lock. Ears hear. A table provides a safe cushion between people, drawing them close, but not too close.

A plate full of food nurtures vulnerability. People are more apt to share and listen when some of their attention is redirected to the simple tasks of passing a platter or buttering a biscuit.

Job loss, engagements, spousal abandonment, cancer diagnoses, pregnancies, business promotions—my table has been the threshing floor for all of these. It's been crowded with opportunities to weep with those who weep and rejoice with those who rejoice (Rom. 12:15). Dinner time has been a conduit for sharing celebrations, service, and sorrow. None of the meals started as interventions or "sharing circles." They were just meals. But intentional hospitality around the table provided the pause necessary to allow others to share in ways they otherwise wouldn't have.

The table's not only a great place to serve but also a place to be served. Practically speaking, the recipes you make and the rituals you keep are tangible ways you can connect cultures and people down through the ages. When you serve up Grandma's chicken tetrazzini or Uncle Joe's BBQ ribs, you are voluntarily laying your past and your family culture in front of those who've pulled up a chair, inviting them into your *familiar*. In that way, serving a meal can leave you feeling exposed. That vulnerability and connectedness is an important aspect of the give-and-take of hospitality. You don't just need to provide hospitality, you need to be able to receive it, even at your own table. Jesus Himself modeled both vulnerability and connectedness. He knew we were never meant to walk this life as lone rangers.

Jesus often used the table to show us the way to community because a meal is a natural equalizer. Everyone needs to eat. Hunger shows no partiality. It touches the rich and the poor, the famous and the infamous. The table is a place for all. A shared meal not only soothes the pain and loss of the widow and orphan but also gives them a place to belong.

I can't help but think of Lisa, a single woman I met at an informational meeting. We were both new to town, struggling to overcome outsider syndrome. I had formed acquaintances with a total of what felt like .2 people at the time, so our introduction more than doubled my social circle. If memory serves, it was at our second happenstance run-in that I invited Lisa over for lunch. To be honest, before the words of welcome even came out of my lips, I had nearly talked myself out of extending them. She was a twenty-something, vibrant professional with a life of endless possibilities and no commitments, no strings, no responsibilities weighing her down. I, on the other hand, was a middle-aged married woman with five exceptionally loud kids. My pantry contained the fixings for grilled cheese sandwiches and little else. My offerings were exceptionally underwhelming, to say the least.

Our tables hold a valuable secret the world longs to know. A meal of bread and wine was God's plan to remind the stranger that He is good and loving and true.

Why in the world would she want to sit at my table? I wondered. *The food quality will be low; the noise level will be high.* Turns out, she was just as desperate for community as I was. Since she'd grown up as the youngest in a rather large family, she was missing the comfort of crowded living. She came. We ate. Slowly a relationship started to form. In time, I invited her to a Bible study I was a part of. It was a hodgepodge collection of outliers, myself included, who had very little in common, save for Christ. She, a single woman who was exploring faith, fit right in.

Our tables hold a valuable secret the world longs to know. A

meal of bread and wine was God's plan to remind the stranger that
He is good and loving and true. Any time we welcome someone
to our table and show them the
hospitality God entrusted to us,
we have an opportunity to meet
their physical need but also to
address the deep spiritual hunger only the Bread of Life can
fulfill. The word *hospitality* stems
from the same Latin root as the
word *hospital*.[8] In that sense, the
very act of opening our doors
and inviting others to the table
can be both preventative and in-
tensive care for humanity. It can provide a natural time and place
for offering them the cure for their sin sickness—Jesus—and as a
natural side effect, we can build a lasting relationship that will live
on through eternity.

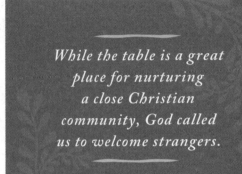

While the table is a great place for nurturing a close Christian community, God called us to welcome strangers.

It's often tempting to set out plates for familiar ones—our
family, our friends, other church members. But while the table
is a great place for nurturing a close Christian community, God
called us to welcome strangers. In our "This seat's taken" society,
let's not forget to leave a few open seats for the wandering ones.
In the words of Jesus, "It is not the healthy who need a doctor, but
the sick. I have not come to call the righteous, but sinners" (Mark
2:17 NIV). Jesus ate with strangers. He ate with sinners. What's
more, He ate with enemies. For His last meal, He invited a man
He knew would betray Him. He sent the invite anyway. Eating
together is a sign of revolution. It unites folks from diverse back-
grounds, nationalities, and affiliations and tells the world that
peace has been made and a family has been formed.

Feeding people in obedience to God's instruction and Christ's example is a spiritual act of worship. It is trusting God and His ways. It's laying down our comfort and any elaborate plans we've made to change the brokenness of the world. It's recognizing that the difference between Christian hospitality and a social gospel is Christ. When we look closely at the way He most often changed lives, we see a simple pattern repeated. Jesus met the need in a person's hand before He met the need in their hearts. He made the lame man walk before He called him to step into righteousness. He saved the physical life of the woman caught in adultery before He showed her the way to a life no longer defined by sin. He filled the fishermen's nets before He called them to fish for men. Christ knew that a "Go and sin no more" message would be drowned out by the rumbling of an empty stomach. So Jesus multiplied fish and loaves. He satisfied physical needs before He met spiritual ones, and in the end, the former almost always paved the way for the latter.

WHAT'S THE HOLDUP?

Hyggelig hospitality recognizes that the table is important but only because of the people gathered around it. The table gives value to all and aims to make those gathered feel better when they leave than when they came, including the host. Recently, I learned how exceptionally cordial this kind of reception truly is. While listening to a widely popular lifestyle podcast, I stood baffled as I heard the co-host describe a "run-in" with her neighbors. They had shown up at her doorstep unannounced, and she found their impromptu visit "invasive." Invasive? Really? What about making people feel better? She went on to say that most people need at least a few days' notice before hosting guests. As a woman who hosts guests at least two times a week, I couldn't imagine that her opinion represented the masses. Surely, her response was the exception and not the rule. Right?

For days I thought about her words. Like a bad country song playing on permanent repeat in my head, I rehearsed the podcast and my feelings about it over and over until I just couldn't stand it anymore. I took to social media to pose one simple question: "Do you find it difficult to invite guests into your home? If so, why?" (Talk about leading the witness.) I hit "publish" fully expecting to receive "Nope. Wanna come over? I've got coffee brewing" as a reply. Like the infamous captain who pronounced the Titanic unsinkable, I could not have been more wrong.

Hundreds of responses began to flood my screen. Women from all around the world, from every walk of life, and every socio-economic status weighed in. Their answer was a resounding, "Yes, it's difficult! I'd like to host people, but I just can't." Confused and a little shell shocked, I began to pull on the thread a bit more. I followed up with many of the commenters and found that while their replies varied, their reservations were all the same. Like that podcast host, these women found hosting others to be imposing for three main reasons.

What if they say no? The threat of rejection is a real possibility. Offering an invitation is a lesson in vulnerability. The practice will often leave you feeling open and exposed. But can I encourage you to send an invite anyway? If that particular person or group of people isn't interested and gives you the brush-off, just consider that offer of hospitality a trial run and try again. Turn to the next person in line. Remember, three out of five people in America are lonely. They, like you, want real and lasting connections. They too fear being dismissed or passed over. Someone has to be brave enough to say, "I'll go first." Will you value the gospel message enough to be the one?

My house is too small. One could also add *too cluttered, too far outside of town, too plainly decorated, too messy, too fill-in-the-blank* to the lengthy list of house transgressions. I get it. For thirteen of the first twenty years of my marriage, I lived in a teeny, tiny 900-square-foot house on the "bad" side of town. My design aesthetic was "pre-owned," which was really just code for "hand-me-down" and "thrifted." It was a perfect starter home, but by the time we moved out, there were seven of us crammed in there. Every day felt like one never-ending game of Sardines.

> If I had waited to invite "the stranger" over until I had the right-sized house or ideally located house, or perfectly decorated house, I'd still be waiting.

But space is like money. No matter how much you have, you'll always think you need more.

If I had waited to invite "the stranger" over until I had the right-sized house or ideally located house, or perfectly decorated house, I'd still be waiting. I had to remind myself that Jesus Himself had nowhere to lay His head. It's not that He had an imperfect house, but that He had no house at all. Even still, He showed us the way to hospitality. Welcoming the stranger is not confined to a beautiful home or even a big home. It can come on a dusty road headed to Emmaus, along the seaside with the smell of rotting fish being washed up on shore, or even the back bench of a fishing boat being tossed about by the winds and waves. Knowing this, I had to find ways to make my micro-space a place where people could gather and the gospel could grow.

Over the years, in addition to the typical one-and-done dinners, family holiday gatherings, and Bible study groups, the furniture in my matchbox-sized living room was repositioned to host women's craft groups, costume parties, and fantasy football drafts; board game nights, support groups, and homeschool co-op classes; book clubs, baby showers, and planning meetings. A hodgepodge mix of folding chairs and card tables were crammed into my dining area to create space for annual cookie exchanges, mother-daughter tea parties, ice cream socials, pumpkin carving parties, a couples-only supper club, and numerous work luncheons. Yard toys were wrangled into the garage to make room for father-son campouts, playdates, backyard Bible clubs, campfire cookouts, and neighborhood block parties. An upstairs loft room was renovated for a troubled teen who needed a place to live. The main level eventually became the occasional backdrop for a small but growing church—a motley crew of wanderers who wanted to know God more but who felt out of place, overlooked, or uneasy in a traditional church building. If I had stretched the walls any further, they would have ripped clean through. My point is, I made my small space work for hospitality because, like the Danes, I make room for what is most important in my life.

The space was small, but no one seemed to mind. The tight quarters made everyone scooch a little closer to one another. It serendipitously forced face-to-face connections and intimate conversations. I'll admit, each time I welcomed people over I couldn't help but wonder if someone else should play hostess—someone with a larger home, a bigger table, a more comfortable couch. In the early days, my invitations almost always started with an awkward preamble, "Just so you know, our home is small." But after years of hosting crowds in my cramped quarters, I've come to realize how unnecessary and self-focused that forewarning is. Your home might feel small. But chances are, your guests won't mind. If we're honest, most of us crave more care and concern than more couch space. Dole out care and concern in lavish ways, and I guarantee no one will feel the least bit crowded.

Hospitality requires too much work. Create a guest list, send invitations, plan a menu, make a playlist, shop for groceries, design a tablescape, unearth and polish the fancy dishes, wash and press the table linens, chill the dessert, prepare the meal, dress for the occasion, light the candles, wash the dishes, do the mopping, "Keep-a busy, Cinderelly!"— perhaps this is the list that churns in your head every time you think about hosting others in your home. If so, no wonder you've stamped "Too much work" over the whole thing. That list is nearly as long as the tax code and would take more than a pack of animated mice to help you complete it.

> *Welcoming the stranger chooses service over performance, present over perfect.*

Might I offer you a word of encouragement I hope will dowse the hot flames of frustration that surround your attempts at hosting? Unless Victorian-era aristocracy has suddenly made a comeback in your neighborhood, you might be making hospitality harder than it needs to be. In chaining yourself to a lengthy list of to-dos, you may inadvertently lose sight of the whole point of hospitality: to welcome the stranger. Don't make the experience about you, make it about them. Remember, Leviticus 19:34 kind of hospitality leads with *'āhaḇ* love. It chooses service over performance, present over perfect.

I realize that for some, no amount of *good-enoughing* will ever feel good enough. Perhaps, like me, you are a "love is in the details" kind of woman. The time, effort, and consideration you give to the table is your way of showing you care. When you pay—in time, talent, or even in finances—you pay attention. That's understandable. I'm wired that way too. But if we're not careful, you and I can easily let perfection turn us into a bunch of draft dodgers, running from that great high call of God to see and know and love the stranger.

Whenever I'm tempted to overcomplicate an invitation, I ask myself these simple questions:

- *Am I thinking about myself—my home, my food, my image—or am I thinking about my guests and what will make them feel loved and welcomed?*

- *Am I scurrying around cleaning, cooking, and preparing to impress them, or is my desire to provide a space that will invite them into my life and the hope I have in God's Son?*

- *Is my goal to entertain or to help others enter into communion with Christ?*

This simple self-assessment of reasons and reservations helps me to recalibrate my attitude and embrace *hyggelig* hospitality.

PRACTICAL HOSPITALITY

Perhaps hospitality already comes easily for you. It feels like a natural extension of your personality and is a natural go-to for showing love. But then again, maybe it isn't. Maybe you're like those many women who responded to my unofficial survey, who feel hospitality is out of reach. You'll be hospitable when you live in a different house or are in a different season of life, you've determined. I urge you not to wait around for ideal conditions or the pipe dream of perfection. There's rarely a right time for welcoming people to your table. Given the option, you'll almost always talk your way out of it and practice procrastination for the rest of your days. Instead, I challenge you to find ways to make hospitality more manageable in your home and during this season. Here are a few practical, *hygge*-like suggestions for your consideration.

Thrifted dishes. At one time and for some strange reason known only to the gift registry department of my local department store, I owned five sets of dishes. Yes, you read that right. I owned five complete sets. They were all seasonally specific and of varying degrees of *fancy*, only one of which was appropriate for everyday use. But over time, pieces of each set became chipped or cracked or lost. At best, I could scrape together an entire table setting of Christmas dishes and enough matching everyday plates to serve five or six. (Did I mention there are seven people in my family?) So, I decided to purge the clutter and switch to all-white dishes. I began picking them up at tag sales, yard sales, and thrift shops for a few pennies each. I brought them home and pieced together an ever-evolving collection of gently used shabby chic tableware.

None of the pieces match in shape or style; my cupboards look like the Land of Misfit Plates. Yet somehow, their lack of color or collective pattern creates a cohesive look. White is universal and can be dressed up or down to fit any occasion. And the best part about a hodgepodge collection is that it's never limiting. I can host as many or as few people as I want. I'm not constrained by set size. Should one piece get broken or cracked by an excited toddler or an unsteady great-grandpa, I can replace it easily for less than a dollar. Everyone's welcome to use "the good dishes" in my home because thrifting helps me prioritize people over property.

Default meal plan. If you're invited to my house for a family-style supper, you should come prepared to eat chicken alfredo with bow-tie pasta, a side salad, and garlic bread. If it's more of a sit on the porch and enjoy a cozy conversation kind of visit, I'll serve you a tall glass of Arnie Palmer (lemonade iced tea). If we're inside by the fire, smothered in blankets, you can expect a mug of coffee and a slice of warm banana bread. Should you invite me to a pot-luck or a pass-a-dish party, you can pencil me down to bring home-made baked mac-n-cheese. Always. This is my default meal plan for hospitality. While I never feel chained to it, especially if a guest has a food allergy or sensitivity, a simple list of potential meals helps me to say yes to hospitality more times than I say no. It frees me from the decision fatigue of menu planning. I can welcome im-promptu visitors because I make it a point to have the ingredients for these recipes on hand at all times. Because I've chosen dishes and drinks I'm very comfortable making, I can easily whip them up while doing other things like chatting with my guests, without getting distracted or overwhelmed. These meals are all brainless crowd-pleasers. Most can be prepared in advance in large batches, divided into smaller quantities, and frozen for later use. So, the next time you saunter up to my door for a quick visit, don't be sur-prised if I duck down to my basement freezer to pull out a mini loaf of banana bread. I'll pop it in the oven to reheat and be almost ready to serve it up by the time you've hung up your coat.

While it might sound boring to always serve the same thing, the truth is, most people are so grateful for something hot and tasty to eat that they never notice what *is* or *is not* included on the menu. Food made and shared with love is always appreciated.

Hospitality budget. You don't have to have deep pockets to show love in tangible ways around the table. The Bread of Life is nourish-ing even when accompanied by peanut butter and jelly. A prayer of corporate thanksgiving can be lifted over lobster or leftovers. I find that I'm more comfortable with hospitality when I allocate for it. Even during our most lean years when there was more month than money, I tried to make our grocery bill a bigger line item in the budget. At times, that meant foregoing weekend take-out or early morning coffee runs. To this day, we rarely go to restaurants, but choose to devote any extra fun-food money to the hospitality column. I can't just give lip service to table ministry. As with all things in life, my wallet reflects what I find most valuable. While my weekly grocery bill has increased, so have my relationships.

Hyggelig hospitality often involves potluck-style meals. If your budget is tight, don't be afraid to ask guests to contribute to the meal. Certain personalities *prefer* to help in some way so as not to leave the host with all the responsibility. Consider creating a charcuterie board—a platter of various meats, cheeses, nuts, fruit, bread, and really anything that can be mixed and matched to form a finger-food-style sample platter. Guests could each be assigned to bring one or two items of their choosing to add to the collective tray.

Build-your-own dinners are another way to assemble a crowd-sourced meal. As the host, you can supply the main ingredient and ask your guests to each bring an item to contribute. Not only are these types of meals easy to prepare, but they're also versatile, especially for those with small children or picky eaters. Similar to a painting, a build-your-own dinner starts with a blank canvas—meat, broth, starch, or grain—created by the host. Each person can then add an assortment of colors, flavors, and textures to their canvas to suit their tastes. It's both a meal and an activity rolled into one.

Doorstep hospitality. Sometimes the best, most sincere form of hospitality is the kind that doesn't require overthinking. It's served up spontaneously and never a burden to the giver or the receiver. When a friend does poorly on a final exam, when your pastor is asked to perform the funeral of a beloved church member, when

GREAT STARTER IDEAS FOR

BUILD-YOUR-OWN MEALS

RICE BOWLS

TORTILLA BAR

ULTIMATE NACHOS

BAKED POTATO BAR

PERSONAL PIZZAS *(pre-made Naan or flatbread makes good individual pizza crusts)*

PASTA BAR

HOAGIES

ICE CREAM SUNDAES

EVERYTHING SOUP *(Guests bring cooked meats, chopped and steamed veggies, and various soup garnishes, with host providing homemade basic hot broth to pour on top)*

your neighbor gets served with divorce papers—these are times when perhaps even an informal dinner invitation would feel overwhelming or stressful to you and to them. A simple and impromptu gesture of hospitality can be delivered right to their door, however, allowing them to immediately taste and see that God is still good and that He still cares for them.

This form of service, while seemingly impulsive, does require a little bit of premeditation. Begin to pay attention to the fun-food preferences of the major players in your life—your friends, family, coworkers, pastor, coaches, teachers, and neighbors. What kind of coffee do they usually order? What snack foods do they grab in the minimart while paying for gas? What ice cream flavor do they consistently order when you're out together? If answering these questions is too difficult to do in stealth mode, don't be afraid to just ask. No one will be offended that you care enough about them to want to know their signature drink. Keep a running list of their names and their favorites on your phone. Then the next time you get wind of their difficult day, you can swing over to their place with a triple-venti, half sweet, nonfat caramel macchiato to show that their pain is seen, that they are seen. For around five dollars, you can provide no-fuss 'āhaḇ.

> The burden and the blessing of hospitality can and should be part of the collective heartbeat of your entire house and all its members.

Hospitality helpers. Hospitality can feel like a strain when all the responsibility is on your shoulders. But, unless you live alone, both the burden and the blessing of hospitality can and should be part of the collective heartbeat of your entire house and all its members, even the youngest ones. When you invite your children into *hyggelig* hospitality and entrust them with a real job that benefits others, you are saying, "Your gifts are needed here. This task, this place, these people need you." They begin to see where their God-given talents and their place in His kingdom work collide. In that way, your home becomes a training ground for the next generation of *hygge* hosts.

Even young children can greet guests at the door, take coats, provide toys and friendship for kid guests, create and display a welcome sign in the driveway or entryway, offer to bring a drink, or show guests to the bathroom as needed. Brainstorming with kids about possible questions they can ask the guests and training them in proper table manners is a kindness you can give them. It helps children feel confident in new social scenarios; it provides them with tangible tools for creating a comfortable and considerate environment for a guest; and it reinforces the fact that children have something to contribute to the relationships being formed.

PRESENCE BEFORE PERFECTION

Hygge provides a means of hosting others without wearing yourself slap-out with a lengthy list of to-dos. It's a belief that people hunger for more than just a great meal, they crave connection. *Hyggelig* hospitality doesn't preclude tidying up or putting your best foot forward. It just means you don't have to feel the need to sterilize your life and wipe out every evidence of brokenness from your home. It means you don't have to secret your real self and your real messes away. It encourages you to share your whole self so your guests feel comfortable enough to do the same.

During one particularly difficult season of relational busyness when I was having trouble finding time to make connections with both friends and strangers, *hygge* hospitality became a life-line. I sent out an appeal on social media to two other women who seemed in a similar state of emotional poverty. I invited them for a bi-weekly playdate of sorts. Like me, those ladies were tired—parched and empty. As moms of many little ones, they were strung out on the drug of efficiency. They needed to find a way to thrive, not just survive, another wearisome winter. What they needed most of all was the gentle kindness of a Savior more than willing to unburden their shoulders if they'd only let Him. A quick consultation of our collective calendars showed we all had a least two weekday mornings a month free from work obligations. So, we formed a plan to spend the fall months in rest together.

With kids in tow, every other Tuesday found us gathered at a home—my home at first, but eventually theirs too as they soon learned to embrace the easy hospitality of *hygge*. We took turns welcoming and being welcomed. We'd slough off our snow boots by the door, pile our coats and mittens in a heap by the closet, and point our kids in the direction of playrooms or game tables.

There was no agenda. Expectations were low. It was always a slow morning filled with talking, laughing, and purposeful care of one another—me with my friends and my kids with theirs. As friendships strengthened, conversations naturally took on deeper and weightier topics such as mounting medical bills and marital trouble. Jesus met us there on the couch every other Tuesday because we were purposeful to save Him a spot.

Somewhere midday, an assembly line was formed. We paused to make lunch. A simple spread of meat and cheese sandwiches on buns, chips, and fruit was the uncomplicated menu every time— no gourmet, no fuss, no decision fatigue. We embraced the scruffy hospitality of *hygge*, overlooking piles of clean but unfolded laundry, breakfast dishes in the sink, and toddlers running around in Superman capes. We spread our arms wide to authentic living because there was safety in numbers. We'd just rest and enjoy being with one another. And that was enough.[9]

Just before He left this earth all those many years ago, Jesus extended an invitation. He is right now preparing a lavish feast for His bride. If you are in Christ, you're not only welcomed at that table, but you have the privilege of welcoming others to it on His behalf. Your home and your table can be where introductions are made. Welcome the stranger. Show them the *'āhaḇ* of God. See them. Know them. Love them with the hospitality of *hygge*.

CONSIDERING HOSPITALITY

1. Was there ever a time when you felt ministered to through a shared meal?

2. What were the best parts of the experience? How did the hosts or meal providers make you feel seen, known, and loved?

3. Do you find hosting people in your home difficult or invasive, and why?

4. What practical changes might you make to make hosting easier and more enjoyable for you?

5. Who in your life is a stranger in need of the *'āhaḇ* love of God?

6. What form of hospitality could you extend to that person in this season of life?

7. Who are the major players in your life? What are their fun-food favorites?

TASTE AND SEE

- Hebrews 13:2
- 1 Peter 4:9
- Romans 12:13
- Luke 14:12–14

———— A PRAYER FOR HOSPITALITY ————

Lord, You have called me to welcome the stranger and to show them Your 'āhab love. Open my eyes to see who in my life needs the companionship of Christ. Reveal to me practical ways to help them feel seen, known, and loved. Don't allow my insecurities or my self-focus to keep me from extending my table to them. May my home be a place where others can not only be fed a meal but also nourished with the Bread of Life. Amen.

RELATIONSHIPS

I believe that appreciation is a holy thing, that when we look for what's best in the person we happen to be with at the moment, we're doing what God does. So, in loving and appreciating our neighbor, we're participating in something truly sacred.

FRED ROGERS

W hen God created the first person on the sixth day, He did something He had not done with any of His prior creation: He talked with Adam. True, God had spoken *to*, *at*, and *about* all creatures, great and small. But talking *with* was reserved for the image-bearer. *With* garnered a blessing. *With* encouraged intimacy. It invited participation. It created conversation, not just commands.

When God created humanity, He wasn't trying to fill a void. God was not lonely, as some scholars have suggested. On the contrary, just as an artist is compelled to paint for the sheer enjoyment of creating, God formed Adam for His own good pleasure. In His triune glory, however, He was well aware of the value of community. God the Father, God the Son, and God the Holy Spirit were the epitome of a healthy relationship and knew Adam couldn't be the only person in this new home. Loneliness would surely result. Genesis 2:18 reads, "Then the LORD God said, 'It is not good that man should be alone; I will make him a helper fit for him.'"

With God's breath still swirling and setting within him, Adam welcomed Eve, a companion ripped right from his side and repositioned to stand beside him for the rest of their days. "At last!" tore from Adam's lips. One singular part—a broken rib—was refashioned to make a whole; the two became one. Alone, neither would be able to enjoy the full perfection of God or His creation. Together, they would have complete access to God and would more fully understand the relationship of the Godhead. Not only that, but their emotional and physical intimacy would reflect the closeness they'd share with their Creator. In this perfect starter home of the Garden, Adam and Eve had every opportunity to build a perfect relationship, one not marred by anger, doubt, fear, or blame. It was here, in the Garden, that the seeds of connection were first planted. Humanity was free to pursue each other and to be pursued by God.

THE RELATIONSHIPS OF JESUS

Genesis 3:8 implies that God walked *with* Adam and Eve in the cool of the evenings. These twilight strolls were just the start of His eternal pursuit of humanity. Even after the Fall, when sin had severed their inimitable communion and separated the created ones from their Creator, leaving them to wander aimlessly covered in shame, God was relentless. He continued to reach for them. He met Moses on a mountain, sent His presence to fill both the tabernacle and the temple, and eventually came down to be God with us, Immanuel.

When sin made it impossible for us to go to Him, God the Son left the wonder of heaven to come to us. From womb to tomb, Jesus showed us the way to *with*-ness. He could have come in any form and within any boundaries. Yet He chose to come in flesh and to be placed in a family. It's difficult to imagine that, in God's sovereignty and with a plan designed since before time began, He thought an ordinary home would be the perfect Garden where this Last Adam could grow best, not just in stature but in favor with God and humankind.

God has veiled these years, leaving us to wonder what it must have been like for a young child Jesus to find His place in the turbulence of a blended family with siblings who didn't always think the best of Him or an adolescent Jesus who humbly set aside His own plans in order to be about His Father's business. In the fullness of His deity, Jesus learned to relate to people in the same way we are tasked to, under the threshold of an ordinary home.

Lest we think Jesus' home was somehow better or more conducive to nurturing loving relationships than ours, let's not forget that apart from Jesus, perfection was in short supply in the small town of Nazareth. According to the apostle Nathaniel, up until that point, nothing good had ever come out of Nazareth. His was a home probably much like yours and mine, filled with more than its share of constant chatter, unmet expectations, broken hearts, rude relatives, disappointments, hurt feelings, stories of unrequited love, tears of frustration, deafening silence, and even raw rage. Nonetheless, it was here, at home, that Jesus learned to call people by name, spend time with them doing what they enjoyed doing, and care enough about their needs to meet them. Home was a greenhouse for relationships. Home was where we see God *with* us, Immanuel.[1]

Like God the Father, Jesus pursued humankind. He drew near to them, stepping into their celebrations and their sorrows. The woman with the issue of blood (Mark 5:25–34) is just one of dozens of examples of how one conversation with Christ changed the entire trajectory of a person's life, not just for eternity, but also for the here and now.

Due to the harsh purity laws inflicted upon the people by the religious elite, this woman had been ostracized from human connection for twelve years. Anything or anyone she came in contact with would have been considered unclean and would have had to be subjected to rigorous cleansing rituals. Scripture does not indicate whether she was married or if she had any children before her diagnosis, but we can assume that if she had immediate family, they'd be unable to comfort or console her in one of the most difficult times in her life lest they risk their own disgrace. She would not have been permitted to participate in temple worship, leaving her no access to God or others for more than a decade. The cultural ramifications of her obvious barrenness, which at that time was thought to be a curse by God and a punishment for sin, would be another stone stacked on her mounting pile of structured shame and loneliness. Her illness may have made her physically anemic, but her lack of relationships made her emotionally, socially, and spiritually anemic.

Like an orphan searching for scraps, this woman slipped into the crowd, hoping to encounter the One who could restore her—to heal not just her body, but her personhood. Ignoring the fallout that would surely come her way for breaking the law, she reached out and touched the hem of Jesus' cloak. Please understand, this simple gesture was no small thing. It took an enormous amount of courage and desperation for her to cast herself on Christ's mercy. At that time, a woman was forbidden to touch in public any man who was not her immediate relative by marriage or birth. By reaching out in this way, the woman knew she was amputating all hope of social standing. But she was desperate. She needed healing. Even more than that, she needed connection.

"Who touched my clothes?" Jesus asked. "'You see the people crowding against you,' his disciples answered, 'and yet you can ask, "Who touched me?"' But Jesus kept looking around to see who had done it. Then the woman, knowing what had happened to her, came and fell at His feet and, trembling with fear, told Him the whole truth. He said to her, 'Daughter, your faith has healed you. Go in peace and be freed from your suffering'" (Mark 5:30–34 NIV).

The law demanded retribution. Jesus chose *relationship* instead. When a forgotten one approached, He didn't run. He didn't overlook. He leaned in. He sought her out. He stepped toward her brokenness, never demanding she clean herself up first. Theirs was a connection unlike any she had experienced before. Jesus was not concerned with what she offered. He cared more about what He could provide. No doubt, she had been called many names in the last twelve years; *daughter* was probably not one of them. In giving her a title that expressed care, protection, and familial connection, Jesus wasn't just naming her, He was renaming her. Jesus was declaring to the world that she was not just acceptable, she was accepted. He was casting a vision for not only what she was, but also what she could be for all eternity. His words gave her life in more ways than one.

Like all people, her relationship with God was broken. In that one brief encounter, Jesus became a necessary bridge builder. Because of His finished work on the cross, all of humanity can now experience that same kind of peace and freedom that comes with Christ's *with*-ness.

The woman with the issue of blood was just one of dozens

of people whose lives were forever changed when confronted by Christ. But what of all the others, the countless multitudes that He never met, that He never healed, that He never renamed? Remember, Jesus was fully human. He came at a particular point in history and was placed among a particular group of people. Confined to flesh, He did not meet every person's relational needs. But Jesus did leave a remnant— the first Christ followers—who could carry on with this mission. In making deep and lasting connections with a few, Jesus was a stone tossed into the tumult, causing a rippling effect for all of eternity. The handful of folks He loved passed that love onto others, who passed it onto others.

> *If you are in Christ, you have been a recipient of a lavish wave of love. Now it's your turn to pass it on to others, to declare the Garden truth:* It is not good for people to be alone.

If you are in Christ, you have been a recipient of that lavish wave of love. Now it's your turn to pass it on to others, to declare the Garden truth: *It is not good for people to be alone.* You're now tasked to show the wounded ones that *separation* and *rejection* don't have to be the anthems of their lives. *Hygge* is a tool that can help you do that.

HYGGE RELATIONSHIPS

As an invitational lifestyle, *hygge* recognizes our basic need to feel connected, to feel a Garden-like *with*-ness with others. *Hygge* therefore encourages deliberate relationships. Despite the fact that in the twenty-first century we are more "connected" than ever, many of us struggle to make the genuine connections that can provide the kind of rescue, redemption, and restoration Jesus offers. For a culture that claims to have mastered social media, we have become the most unsocial generation in all of history, and the repercussions of that physical and emotional separation is staggering.

According to the National Institute of Health Care Management, loneliness is a health crisis in America, increasing the potential of premature death to equal that of smoking and obesity.[2] Some studies show that as many as 60 percent of American adults over eighteen report feeling left out, misunderstood, and lacking companionship.[3] How can we have instant access to anyone at any time with just a simple tap of an app and yet feel so completely alone? Could it be we have replaced friendships with "friends"? Genuine love for "likes"? The common bond built over a shared meal around a table with a "shared" meme on a tablet? While the blame for our loneliness can't be solely placed on the digital devils we carry around in our pockets, the correlation between the decrease in our face-to-face interactions and the increase in our feelings of isolation and abandonment are worth noting.

Because it prioritizes a slower pace, *hygge* can free us from our everyday distractions and encourage us to be present in the moment—to participate in quality time and meaningful conversations with those we love or those who need our love. *Hygge*, like its name implies, is like a hug.

A *hyggelig* relationship is one in which participants feel equally valued and that their voice matters and will be heard. In *The Book of Hygge*, Louisa Thomsen Brits writes, "Danes have a strong cultural aversion toward aggressive behavior and cooperate to avoid contentious issues or divisive topics."[4] There are times when engaging in difficult discourse is necessary, however. *Hygge* doesn't mean we should stay on the surface or overlook complex or weighty issues;

it just means that even our hard conversations should be engaging and inclusive.

Relationships are built with familiarity in mind, which means, like Jesus during His earthly ministry, the Danes don't seek to make connections with everyone. Instead of casting their social nets broadly, unwittingly building relationships a mile wide but only an inch deep, they narrow their focus and have tighter societal circles and rich, lasting connections. Danes are not preoccupied with social class and material excess, so *hygge* allows for even the least of these to be welcomed and enveloped with love. Showing off and one-upping have no place in their lives. Like Jesus, people practicing *hygge* can build the kind of meaningful alliances that create a rippling effect, sending waves of friendship and *with*-ness to the rest of the world.

In its *us* over *me* posture, *hygge* encourages shared experiences and relaxing activities with family and friends. *Fredagshygge*, or Friday family nights, is one intentional way the Danes have learned to build familial bonds with others and to quiet the chaos and noise of cultural distractions.[5] During *Fredagshygge*, Danes forgo elaborate plans and choose instead to enjoy simple pleasures like playing a board game or watching a movie together. In saying yes to *hygge*, they grant themselves permission to say no to work, worries, and mental stress.

REASONS TO RELATE

In a candid television interview, Nebraskan senator and *New York Times* bestselling author, Ben Sasse, reported that Americans have gone from an average of 3.2 close friends to 1.8, and 40 percent of our neighbors have fewer than one confidant in their lives.[6] He went on to say that Americans used to be able to disagree with one another and still be friends because we were friends first. But with our collapse of social capital—of neighbors gathering on the porch or chatting over the backyard fence—cultural polarization has become an epidemic in this country, creating a great divide between races, classes, and genders. One obvious by-product of this relational separation is loneliness.

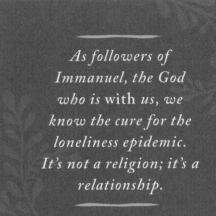

As followers of Immanuel, the God who is with *us, we know the cure for the loneliness epidemic. It's not a religion; it's a relationship.*

If those first few scenes in the Garden taught us anything, it was that people were not meant to be alone. Unfortunately, the enemy is well aware of the power of social separation and will gladly dangle whatever forbidden fruit necessary to isolate us and convince us we are alone.

As followers of Immanuel, the God who is *with* us, we know the cure for the loneliness epidemic. It's not a religion; it's a relationship. Because of Christ, separation has been removed and our intimacy with God has been made possible. In reading that, you might be tempted to conclude that an introduction to Jesus is all your lonely neighbors need in order to be relationally restored. But while a relationship with Christ is the most important antidote for both social and emotional poverty, it's not the entirety of God's plan for curing what ails us. He calls humanity into fellowship with Him, but also with others.

Just before His ultimate betrayal in the garden at Gethsemane, Jesus delivered a powerful message about the *with*-ness created in the original Garden. He said, "This is my commandment, that you love one another as I have loved you" (John 15:12). His desire was that out of the overflow of His love for us, we might show love to others. Our "one another" connections are important in kingdom work. So much so that the words "one another" are mentioned more than fifty times in the New Testament. In each instance, we're urged to reveal the love of Christ by the way we relate to one another, to display God to the world by the way we build relationships.

Psalm 68:6 reminds us that "God sets the lonely in families" (NIV). At one time you and I were both lonely ones. God's given us a place in His family, and now He asks that we make room for others. He invites us to be His ambassadors, to be ministers to loneliness. If we're willing, our homes can be a much-needed welcome mat for a lost and lonely world.

Jesus' life taught us an important lesson about how we should go about nurturing *with*-ness with others: our relationships aren't just about our personal happiness. Our relationships are actually about our sanctification and the salvation and sanctification of others. Jesus built His connections in concentric circles. God the Father was at the center, but He was not the only relationship in Christ's life. Peter, James, and John—a tight band of brothers—were placed in the next loop. An additional nine disciples and partners of ministry found a position in the third circle. A larger band of apostles showed up in the loop just after

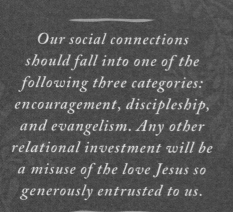

Our social connections should fall into one of the following three categories: encouragement, discipleship, and evangelism. Any other relational investment will be a misuse of the love Jesus so generously entrusted to us.

that. Multitudes appeared in the outer ring. His relationships had a rippling affect.

In curating these circles, Jesus was reinforcing two basic ideas we all should remember when relating to others. The first is this: the cure for loneliness isn't more relationships but deeper ones. And the second? Like in the life of Christ, our social connections should fall into one of the following three categories: encouragement, discipleship, and evangelism. Any other relational investment will be a misuse of the love He so generously entrusted to us when He said, "By this all people will know that you are my disciples, if you have love for one another" (John 13:35).

Encouragement. Like Jesus, you and I need a Peter, James, and John in our lives—a close-knit group of family or friends we encourage and are encouraged by. We need a small tribe of people who have placed God at the center of their concentric circles and who, like Ecclesiastes 4:12 mentions, will help us form a strong, unbreakable cord against the enemy.

My cord has three strands: Emily, Jacqui, and me. That's not to say I don't have other close friendships, but these two women are like heart-sisters to me. We've welcomed babies together, potty-trained toddlers together, sat in hospital rooms together, buried family members together, shared vacations together, launched kids into college together, and cared for aging parents together. We've clapped and cried, celebrated and struggled together. They are not sisters by birth, but because of Jesus, they are sisters by blood. These are the ones who come in without knocking, who know where I keep the extra silverware, who have seen me in a bathing suit, who reach for my clean laundry basket and just start folding while we're talking. These two women are like sweatpants in a sea of skinny jeans. They are my comfort food.

When I'm with Emily and Jacqui, I can't help but draw near to

God because wherever He is, that's where they want to be too. As Proverbs 27:17 says, they are like iron, sharpening me while I'm sharpening them. Our triune relationship has not always been an easy one. We've had more than our share of harsh words and hurt feelings. Curating the kind of friendship that bears the scars of hard-fought *with*-ness has taken an aggressive amount of vulnerability. I had to be brave enough to show up as me, not the *me* I thought I was supposed to be or the *me* the world tells me to be, but the *me* I actually am—the me who is broken but blood-bought, the *me* who knows that wounds from a friend are trustworthy (Prov. 27:6), the *me* who is not only willing to love but to be loved, the *me* who isn't just looking for a relationship that will make me happy, but one that will make me holy.

Ours has been a persistent friendship. It's had to be. Half-in allegiances don't hold when you're trying to build a relationship that will mean something. In an age when the word *friend* feels trivial, cliché, or like a social accessory, these friends of mine saturate me with love—both theirs and God's. They encourage me in my gifts and kingdom callings. They rebuke me when I choose the easy way instead of the righteous way. They overlook my faults while also reminding me that with Christ's help I can do better. "I'm sorry" and "I forgive you" come easily to their lips. Whenever I'm with them, I always feel the touch of Christ on my life.

What about you? Who are your Emily and Jacqui? Do you have a Peter, James, and John in your life—friends you can go to for comfort, encouragement, and hope? Friends who, like Aaron and Hur of Exodus 17:8–16, may not always be able to hold up the staff of victory for you but who are more than willing to hold up your arms while you're doing the work? Do you have friends who know you enough to "No" you—to say the hard things, to tell you when you are out of line, to point out seeds of sin in your life?

On the flip side, are you a *hygge* sister to someone else? Are there women in your life who rely on your encouragement? I know it's not always easy to put yourself out there and invite other women into your life. As I've mentioned before, invitational living can often leave you exposed to potential rejection. But encouragement is not a luxury to the Christian life; it is a necessity. We're often tempted to lump encouragement in with things like a pat on the back or an "Attagirl." But encouragement

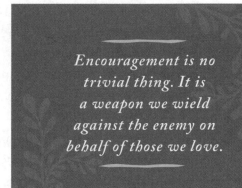

Encouragement is no trivial thing. It is a weapon we wield against the enemy on behalf of those we love.

is more than just giving a compliment. It is the passing on of courage. To encourage someone is to give them the courage to face an unknown future, the courage to trust an unseen God, the courage to stand firm in a turbulent culture. Encouragement is no trivial thing. It is a weapon we wield against the enemy on behalf of those we love. Who is receiving courage from you today?

Discipleship. Like Jesus, you and I also need a small circle of discipleship connections. I like to call these our Mother-Sister-Daughter relationships. That's not to say we have to have biological mothers, sisters, and daughters to experience the fullness of discipleship, but we should have figurative mothers, sisters, and daughters who share our love for Christ and who will act as our generational bloodline of faith.

Titus 2:3–5 commands, "Older women likewise are to be reverent in behavior, not slanderers or slaves to much wine. They are to teach what is good, and so train the young women to love their husbands and children, to be self-controlled, pure, working at home, kind, and submissive to their own husbands, that the word of God may not be reviled." We ought always to reach ahead to an older mother figure of the faith who has hard-won experience to share with us. Additionally, we need to reach across to other women at a similar phase of the journey as we are. We need to link arms with them as sisters in Christ to offer them accountability and care. Last, this passage implies that we should reach back to younger women or new believers in Christ to help pull them along, forging a path of faith for them by our example.

Truly, discipleship can be messy. Like encouragement, there's an element of vulnerability and transparency involved. Discipleship requires longevity. It forces you to admit your fears, faults, and failures, and it demands that you overlook these qualities in others. But developing this ring of relationships doesn't have to leave you with an overdrawn emotional account. The simple recipe for discipling mothers, sisters, and daughters in the faith begins and ends with love—the kind of love shown in small acts, not grand gestures; the kind of love done best in work clothes, not your Sunday best; the kind of love that is faithful, not flashy.

When Christ leaned into the lives of particular people in Scripture, He often showed up in their ordinary moments: a woman sitting at the well, men fishing on the sea, a tax collector counting his coins. Jesus didn't shrink or look away from their messy, work-in-progress lives. As Immanuel, He was the God who stayed, the God who was with them. Let's show Jesus to the world by loving them well in their everyday lives. Let's show them what it looks like when someone stays.

The home is the perfect starting line for discipleship. Unfortunately, our culture often undermines the value of the home. Keeping a home is often viewed as a burden to a woman's personal and professional progress. While most Christian women understand that homemaking is part of our God-given responsibility, if we're being honest, we are often guilty of displaying a radical love for the world outside our walls while completely ignoring the people in it.

We can easily become lazy or indifferent to the work of home discipleship, naïvely believing spiritual training is the job of the pastor, elders, or church elite. Matthew 28:16–20 makes it clear, however, that discipleship is a part of the commission Jesus gave to all His followers—that includes you; that includes me. The reality is, if you've been a Christian for longer than a minute, you are discipling someone. It's not a question of whether or not you are going to disciple them, it's *how* you are going to do it. More is caught than taught. One way or another, those in your home will catch what you are lobbing out, for better or worse.

Do the people in your house see you modeling the fruit of the Spirit? Have you shown them what it looks like to love those who seem unlovely? Discipleship is proactive. It's less about training others to fear doing the wrong thing and more about showing them your love for doing the right thing. It isn't about controlling an outward action; it's about influencing an inward attitude. Others must see you have joy, even in hard and painful things. They should witness you choosing peace when it would be easier

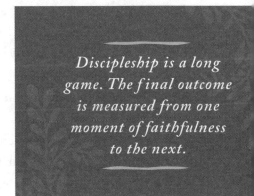

Discipleship is a long game. The final outcome is measured from one moment of faithfulness to the next.

for you to dish out criticism and contempt. God's way up begins when you get down, when you humble yourself, especially in front of those who know you best. If you want to help those in your home grow in spiritual fruit, then you need to provide them with a pattern.

Discipleship is a long game. The final outcome is measured from one moment of faithfulness to the next. Are you showing newer believers the way of faith? Are you growing in discernment and biblical literacy by being in the Word regularly? Are you training others in right living by choosing to live a holy and righteous life, or do you have competing priorities? Are you teaching correct theology by sharing with others your knowledge of who God is and what He has done? Are you encouraging the body in service and in giving by providing the example in your own life? Again, this is lifelong work.

It's sometimes hard to see the years ahead, especially when we let feelings of imperfection get in the way. Our past sins, new and inexperienced faith, or perceived lack of spiritual qualifications can become like a pebble in our shoe, crippling our efforts of discipleship. Carrying around the guilt and shame of a forgiven past is like carrying a backpack full of boulders. Perfection isn't possible on this side of heaven, but with the help of the Holy Spirit, progress is. Others don't need you to be a perfect example of Christlikeness. Your goal is not for them to be *your* disciple, after all. They need you to point them to the One who is worthy of following. The daily battles of discipling may make you wonder whether you're toiling in vain. But keep pressing in. You can't expect a harvest during planting season. Concentrate on reaching the heart of those you've built relationships with, and time will take care of the rest.

You will get relationship interactions wrong occasionally. You will disciple imperfectly. You will make mistakes, lose your cool, reveal your ugly brokenness. But allow God to fill in the gaps. Be willing to hold out your discipleship to the Lord. Ask Him to help you walk in Truth, to be openhanded to the poor, and to be rich in good deeds. Call upon Him to convict you toward loving your enemies, growing in grace, serving with eagerness, and imitating

Jesus with boldness. Imagine the world change that might take place if we did the knee-bending work of prayer for our homes, for ourselves, if we spent just as much time praying as we do providing Pinterest-worthy memories. If we want to ready others to be useful for the Lord and His purposes and callings in their lives, we'd do well to seek God's help in our discipling.

Evangelism. In bearing fruit through discipleship, you'll also produce seeds that will continue the work long after you're gone. This is evangelism, the third and final tier of our relational rings. This is the social circle represented by the fellowship of the multitudes who gathered around Christ, the people whose lives were transformed through the saving power of His message and later His resurrection.

In Christian circles, we often associate the word *fellowship* with a place, as in the Fellowship Hall, or the room in the church basement where coffee and donuts are served. But in the early church, Christians devoted themselves to the action of fellowship—to nurturing a well-rooted community of believers inviting those outside of their faith to learn more about who Christ was and what He had done on their behalf. This kind of inclusivity was a form of *hygge*. It brought people from death to life.

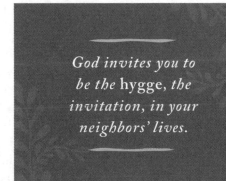

God invites you to be the hygge, *the invitation, in your neighbors' lives.*

As we follow the examples in Scripture for building relationships with the multitudes, we need to remember that the gospel was spread because a handful of faithful men and women told both their friends and their enemies, who in turn did the same (1 Cor. 11:2; 2 Thess. 2:15).

Your neighbors long to be loved without condition. As one who's already been washed in the grace of God through the blood of His Son, you now have the privilege of pointing others to the love that has no end. God invites you to be the *hygge*, the invitation, in their lives.

As we saw in the story of the woman with the issue of blood, Jesus never cherry-picked who He loved. He never demanded people get themselves together first. His message was, "Come as you are" and then "Go and sin no more." He didn't intentionally leave out, forget, or overlook anyone, no matter how unworthy they seemed. Likewise, everyone you meet is a rough draft of the final story God is writing for their life. For some, the first few chapters are messier than others. These people are hard to love and even harder to like. But here's the thing: love is not an option for we who are in Christ. Scripture never says to love if you feel like it or love those you find lovely. It says, "Love one another." Period. Every human being bears the image of the Creator and should receive the dignity this image demands. Whether or not we naturally like a person, the Lord made and loves that person. In fact, our love for God is reflected best in how we love the person we like the least.

Let's not forget on the night before He died, Jesus knelt and washed the feet of Judas, the man who would ultimately betray Him. Knowing this should allow us to extend kindness even when it isn't necessarily deserved in the moment. It should prompt us to live out the full commission of Acts 1:8, "But you will receive power when the Holy Spirit has come upon you, and you will be my witnesses in Jerusalem and in all Judea and Samaria, and to the end of the earth." This passage obviously refers to geographical boundaries, but it also calls attention to the different types of people within them.

It's relatively enjoyable to relate to those in our Jerusalem. These are our family and friends—the people most like us. They often share our lifestyle and hold to a similar worldview, but they may not yet have a saving knowledge of Jesus. Our relationships within our Jerusalem are relatively uncomplicated and easy.

Those in our Judea are somewhat less relatable because they hang out in our broader communities. We often know these folks on a less personal level, perhaps in the workplace, through school events, or while sipping a latte at the coffee counter on Saturday morning. These are our small-talk people, our budding-friendship people.

Jerusalem and Judea are doable. We can relate to them. It's the folks who land in our Samaria category who are the most troubling. They're the ones who make us bristle. Samaritans are our outliers, the people who hold different ideological views and who sit on the other side of the aisle. These are the Democrats or the Republicans. They are those in the LGBTQ community, the Muslims, the immigrants. From the Pharisees to the atheists in our lives, Jesus' command to love is all-inclusive.

To be clear, a gospel without repentance of sin is not the gospel. If you fully understand what salvation saved you from, then you also know that showing love without the full truth of the gospel is not really loving. But your job is not to convict hearts. If memory serves, Jesus did not say, they shall know you by your eloquent sermons, wagging fingers, or political strong-arming. He said they'll know you by your love. You're tasked with the invitation, the love—the *hygge*. Acceptance does not equal approval. After all, Matthew 5:47 reminds us, "If you greet only your friends, what's so great about that? Don't even unbelievers do that?" (CEV). Building relationships with your Samaria just means you've learned how to open your door wide enough to allow anyone to come in and meet the Savior. It just means you're willing to be a Monday minister of reconciliation.

LEARNING TO RELATE

In Philemon 6, we read that by sharing our faith in all our rings of relationships we'll grow in the "full knowledge" of God. In other words, we'll know more of God's love by loving others. We'll understand more about His generosity by giving generously to those in need. We'll be able to experience more *with*-ness with Him as we spend time with those He has created. All of life this side of the first Garden is preparing us for our lives in the second Garden, our final home in heaven as the bride of Christ. You might even say it's premarital counseling. We're learning to love Him more as we love those He's placed around us, as we encourage, disciple, and evangelize.

But while relationships are a part of the collective heartbeat of the Godhead, they're not always easy to begin or to maintain. As a grown adult who still sometimes feels lonely even when I know I'm never really alone, I find that relating doesn't always feel natural. I'm a very awkward human. Whenever I'm in a new social setting, I make a silent vow not to be one of those people who talks too loudly or hugs too tightly. But inevitably, those flimsy promises blow apart the moment I make my introductions. At times, it feels like everyone has learned all the relationship secrets but me. If only forging friendships in adulthood could be as easy as it was when we were kids—when tight alliances were made in the cafeteria over pudding cups, when life problems could all be shared and solved by sundown during a neighborhood kickball game. Now nurturing relationships can often feel like a cycle of madness. An innocent conversation with a lifelong friend can quickly take a weird turn, leaving you feeling like you've just been kicked in the shins. A happenstance interaction with a stranger in the produce aisle can make you scramble for the closest escape hatch.

Hygge, with its no-fuss approach to community-building, can serve as a simple framework for our relational rings. Here are three Danish-like practices that have been especially helpful in my own life as I've sought to replicate Garden-like *with*-ness with those around me.

Questions and answers. Perhaps it's just my own misaligned opinion, but the world seems to have more than enough classes in public speaking. What we need is a public-listening class. *Hygge* is a tool that can help us learn to stop talking all the time. *Hyggelig* living encourages meaningful dialogue instead of short answers in clipped tones. It supports face-to-face connections and handwritten notes over social media posts and direct messages. Feelings of safety are paramount in *hygge,* especially in the realm of relationships. People want to know you are not just listening but you are also hearing them. In *The Little Book of Hygge,* author Meik Wiking writes, "Hygge is an indication that you trust the ones you are with and where you are."[7] You can nurture *hyggelige* conversations by learning to ask great questions and listening intently to the answers people give and the stories they have to share.

In an attempt to disciple my children toward asking good questions and becoming better listeners, I always open our dinnertime discussion by asking one or two open-ended questions:

- What are you grateful for today?
- Who did you serve today?
- How did you fail or succeed today?

Because the questions can never be answered with just a *yes* or a *no*, they draw the conversation in a different direction every single evening. In this way, I'm not only helping my kids develop and practice basic table manners so that mealtime doesn't end up feeling like a pirate uprising, but I'm also strengthening sibling relations and building trust. The children feel free to share because I've made space and time for them to practice sharing. That same level of intentional exchange can also be applied in other relationships.

The power of a perfectly placed question, sincerely asked, can bolster feelings or repair tender wounds for encouragement, clarify a belief or need for discipleship, and open the gates of communication for evangelism. Only a fool takes pleasure in expressing her own opinion (Prov. 18:2). The wise woman, on the other hand, asks good questions. She's quick to hear and slow to speak (James 1:19).

Questions are especially helpful when a conversation has been layered with tension or when lines have been drawn in the relational sand. The next time you're in a verbal tussle and the vein in your temple is beginning to bulge, put down your fighting words and toss out a good question instead. While you're hearing the answer, resist the urge to reload. Your conversations shouldn't resemble a street fight. Spewing vitriol might get someone's attention, but it won't do anything to change their mind. Remember, your ultimate, eternal goal is not to prove your point but to understand someone else's even more. Keep asking questions, and then be willing to lean in and listen to the answers.

The following are open-ended questions that can jumpstart good conversation and promote healthy *hygge*:

- What are you most excited about or disappointed with lately?
- What do you value most in a friend or a friendship?

- What is your biggest strength or struggle?

- How can I pray for you today?

- What do you wish people would know or understand about you?

- What are you most proud of and why?

- Who or what has been the biggest influence in your life?

- What do you wish more people would care about and why?

- What do you know for sure?

- What is the best piece of advice you've ever been given and how has it influenced your life?

- What upsets you most about this present culture? What makes you the most excited about it?

- What do people value most about you?

- What brings you joy?

If yours is a new or budding friendship, don't attempt to bang someone over the head with a Bible verse or use Scripture as the silver-bullet answer for all their problems. You might be very eager to see another person come to saving faith in Jesus or to point his or her life in a direction of peace, but as Theodore Roosevelt is supposed to have said, "No one cares how much you know, until they know how much you care."[8] There is no fast track to trust. Questions show you care. More often than not, people will be more willing to listen to you as they respond to your willingness to listen to them. In time, the conversational bridges you've built can lead to the next level of questions, ones that might help walk them toward the Savior.

The following are open-ended questions that might launch a gospel-centered conversation:

- What comes into your mind when you think about God?
- How do you see God at work in your life right now?
- What is your standard of truth? How do you know if something is right or wrong?
- How much would you sacrifice for someone else? Which person or people do you think deserves that sacrifice?
- Do you deserve someone else's sacrifice? Why or why not?
- Would you consider yourself a good person? Why or why not?
- To you, who was Jesus?
- If you were to die today, what do you think would happen to your soul?
- If God were to ask you, "Why should I let you into heaven?" how would you answer Him?

Service and sacrifice. According to author Marie Tourell Søderbergh, *hygge om* is another layer to Danish living that can yield an avalanche of personal connection for the rest of us.[9] Søderbergh writes that *hygge om*, or providing *hygge* for others, is shown in both big and small ways. Sometimes making *hygge* might require heroic acts of physical sacrifice or generous financial assistance. More often than not, however, the demands on your time and wallet will be rather low stakes, like watching your coworker's cat when she's out of town for the weekend, raking the lawn of your elderly neighbor after his outpatient surgery, or leaving a note of thanks and encouragement along with your tip when it looks like the barista is overworked and understaffed. *Hygge om* will look like simple service but will sound like the language of love.

When you and I are willing to set aside our wants, our plans, our lives for the sake of others, we are reflecting the compassion of Jesus and expressing our deep affection for Him. Christ said "I love you" first. Service to others is one way we declare our love and our *with*-ness in return. Matthew 25:35–40 says, "For I was hungry and you gave me something to eat, I was thirsty and you gave me something to drink, I was a stranger and you invited me in, I needed clothes and you looked after me, I was in prison and you came to visit me" (NIV). Service, or providing *hygge* for others, can be the very lifeblood of your relationships, drawing you closer to God as you draw closer to each other.

Rituals and traditions. *Hygge* opens our eyes to the value of the mundane within our relationships. It observes and celebrates the everyday and turns the tedious into tradition. Because it embraces repetition and elevates routines, *hyggelig* living orders our affections. It echoes the cry of Matthew 6:21, which reads, "Where your treasure is, there will your heart be also." It helps us learn to love the daily rituals we've created with the people we spend the most time with and helps us to see that the whole of our lives is greater than the sum total of all the individual moments.

The cup of coffee we sip with our roommate at the breakfast table each morning, the quick chat with a coworker as we share an elevator on our way into the office, the smile-and-wave we offer to the playground supervisor each afternoon while sitting in the pickup line—these all become a daily liturgy. We no longer begrudge the monotony of a routine life because *hygge* compels us to find the extra of each ordinary moment. In the words of author

Annie Dillard, "How we spend our days, is, of course, how we spend our lives."[10]

Hyggelig living elevates the ordinary but also places a high value on traditions. Traditions are nostalgic and take us back to simpler times. They act as connective tissue between generations, giving us a history and a sense of belonging. They allow us to look backward in order to move forward. They strengthen family and friendship bonds because they're unifying. They offer relational comfort and security, teach the core values of a faith or a national heritage, and create rhythms and seasons to our days. Inviting someone to share in our traditions is inviting them into the story of our lives.

If we're intentional to invite God into our traditions, the traditions can serve to encourage, disciple, and evangelize so the next generation will know of the praiseworthy deeds of the Lord and can tell their children (Ps. 78:1–7). *Hygge* allows us to create a human chain of memories, linking us to one another and eventually to God.

Like the Danish *Fredagshygge*, or Friday family nights, our *hyggelige* traditions don't have to be elaborate and Pinterest-worthy. They can be as simple as always inviting a group of friends over on the first big snowfall to make snow cream together; creating an annual booklet of all the Christmas cards you've received in the mail during the holidays to pray for each of those individuals throughout the year; or passing out popsicles to the kids on your block as they disembark the bus on the last day of school each spring. *Hyggelige* traditions invite others into a shared experience and help us nurture *with*-ness.

The Christian faith is a relationship. It connects us to God through Christ and compels us to connect with others as His ambassador of love and life. *Hygge*, with its obvious emphasis on people over production, belonging over belongings, is a tool we can use to introduce others to the Garden-like intimacy they crave. Its invitational living can provide practical ways for us to encourage, disciple, and evangelize. Like the woman with the issue of blood, our neighbors are lonely. They long to be accepted and restored into fellowship. When we *hygger*, we can introduce them to Immanuel, the God who is *with* us.

──── CONSIDERING RELATIONSHIPS ────

1. Examine your top ten relationships. Which of the three relational rings (encouragement, discipleship, evangelism) do they each represent?

2. What can you do today to encourage someone in your first ring? To disciple someone in your second ring? To share the good news of the gospel with someone in your third ring?

3. If one or more of the rings is not represented, what steps can you take to begin to cultivate relationships in those areas?

4. Which of the three rings is the hardest for you to nurture? Why?

5. How are you serving those in your community? In your local church? In the global church?

6. Which simple traditions could you invite your friends and neighbors to experience with you this season?

──── TASTE AND SEE ────

- 1 Thessalonians 5:11
- Ecclesiastes 4:9–12
- 1 Peter 4:8–10
- Matthew 28:18–20
- 2 Corinthians 5:20

———— A PRAYER FOR RELATIONSHIP ————

God in heaven, You are a triune God of relationship. You have said that it's not good for people to be alone and so You gave us each other. Open my eyes to see who in my life needs encouragement, discipleship, or evangelism. Bring specific names to mind and give me ideas for how to make those connections. Help me begin to grow new relationships by learning to ask good questions, serve others with humility, and invite friends into my home traditions. Set a lonely one in my family. Amen.

WELL-BEING

Resolve to be tender with the young, compassionate with the aged,
sympathetic with the striving, and tolerant of the weak and the wrong.
Sometime in life you will have been all of these.

LLOYD SHEARER

W hen God made room for Adam and Eve in His Garden home, He made sure they were protected, cared for, and given all they needed for personal success and happiness. Then they sinned—and all of that changed. Depravity, destruction, injustice, and bondage—the handmaidens of death crept in. Cloaked in guilt and yet completely naked, save for a few fig leaves, they hid. God could have left them there, separated from Him and doomed to die, but He didn't. Instead, He went to them when they needed Him most.

"Where are you?" He called, already knowing exactly where Adam and Eve were hiding. This was an attempt to draw them out of their shame, to bring them out from behind the barrier of trees. It was for their own well-being that He wanted to show them how distanced they were from Him now because of their disobedience. Care grows through connection. When Adam and Eve were separated from God through sin, their lives were no longer very good. Caring for themselves and for each other became much harder than God had designed it to be.

THE WELL-BEING OF JESUS

From that point forward, death has lurked in the shadows, desolating and destroying the good of the Garden life. To some degree, all of humanity now struggles with self-worth. Sin altered our relationships with both God and His other image-bearers. One of our greatest needs is to regain a sense of value for ourselves and for our friends and neighbors. And that's where Jesus comes in. God sent His Son to restore what was lost in the Garden that day—to return us to life, point us back to our original purpose, declare both peace and victory, bring about justice, and reinstate order. He came to make us well and give us worth. He came so that we can have life—and have it more abundantly (John 10:10).

Obviously, so much of Christ's redemptive work happened because of His death, but let's not forget that redemption came through His life too. All throughout His earthly ministry, Jesus showed us the way to being well—to care for self and to care for others.

Fully human, Jesus knew the importance of taking care of His physical, emotional, mental, and spiritual health. Like all of us, He had only one life to live here on earth. The Gospel accounts reveal how He maintained healthy boundaries with others in order that He could be fully able to do whatever God asked of Him. He developed a habit of prayer and devoted Himself to the meditation and memorization of the Hebrew Scriptures (Mark 1:35; Matt. 14:23;

Luke 6:12). Jesus also practiced gratitude by thanking God for His timely revelation, provision, and attention (Matt. 11:25–27; Matt. 15:36; John 11:41–43).

Scripture also makes it clear that Christ removed Himself from the noise and busyness of a demanding life to rest. While He certainly could have spent every moment healing more people, training more disciples, restoring more brokenness, He didn't. At times He withdrew for solitude. Constrained by flesh, He knew the value of carving out time to quiet His soul. Yet He also never allowed His desire for alone time to eclipse the will of the Father. Mark 6:32–34 records how Jesus was quick to lay down His original plans for self-care, yielding His "rights" in order to serve those around Him: "So they went away by themselves in a boat to a solitary place. But many who saw them leaving recognized them and ran on foot from all the towns and got there ahead of them. When Jesus landed and saw a large crowd, he had compassion on them, because they were like sheep without a shepherd. So he began teaching them many things" (NIV).

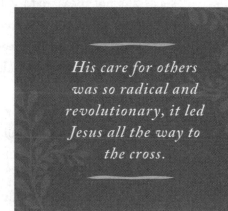

His care for others was so radical and revolutionary, it led Jesus all the way to the cross.

Jesus cared enough to take care of Himself in order that He could care for others. No one was too out of reach for His touch. He gave the marginalized unprecedented dignity. He provided for the poor, restored the identity of prostitutes and tax collectors, served lepers, touched and healed broken bodies. At a time when the rest of the world was hostile toward women, viewing them as nothing more than property, Jesus elevated them. They were not even allowed to speak in public, and yet it was through the testimony of a group of women that the rest of the disciples learned of His resurrected body. Jesus exposed the inhumanity of the religious elite and ignored the social and racial prejudices of the day by forming friendships with Samaritans and Gentiles. His care for others was so radical and revolutionary, it led Jesus all the way to the cross. Because of His sacrifice, the well-being of the Garden will one day be restored.

HYGGE WELL-BEING

Woven tightly into all the other six tenets of *hygge*, well-being is at the very center of Danish living. One cannot feel fully cared for or fully care for others without giving and receiving things like hospitality, relational love, comfort, contentment, and rest. Everything about *hyggelig* living is dedicated to care.

As an egalitarian society, Denmark understands that a nation's success is not measured by its Gross Domestic Product or economic growth but by the well-being of its people. This confirms what social scientists have realized for years. In one of the world's longest-running studies of adult life, begun in 1938 and continuing into the present day, Harvard researchers found that with the exception of extreme poverty, well-being is more connected with a person's relationships, overall health, and meaningful experiences than with their wealth.[1] Touted as having one of the most generous welfare programs in the world, it's no wonder that Denmark boasts a poverty level of only 12.5 percent.[2] *Hyggelig* living helps them downplay social differences and economic disparity in order that they may promote the general well-being of all.[3]

It could certainly be argued that there are many negative social repercussions for wealth redistribution and that welfare is best entrusted to the generosity of individual people rather than the policymakers of a government. While that might be so, the remarkable well-being of the Danish people should inspire us all to take and give care, perhaps not by way of law but certainly by the compulsion of love.

In addition to their rather generous public relief programs, the Danes prioritize physical, emotional, and mental health with plenty of outdoor recreation to stimulate both their bodies and their minds. Time spent out of doors, moving in nature, directly impacts their overall well-being.

Denmark is a compact country, nearly surrounded by water. Since communities are small and since the distances between them are short, the Danish people can often be found walking, biking, or taking public transit in order to experience the fresh air of the coast and the seasonal beauty of nature. These outdoor rituals help them internally relax, reflect, and shake off the lethargy of the day. Most importantly, though, it helps them appreciate their external circumstances and the gift that nature is. When something is a part of a person's everyday life, he or she is more apt to fight for it and take care of it. It's no longer just a policy, it's a personal value. That includes nature but it also includes so much more.

As in the life of Christ, the well-being of *hygge* falls under two categories: self-care and group care. To the Danes, these two forms of care are inseparable; you can't have one without the other.

SELF-CARE

Contrary to the popular "You deserve it!" messages, self-care isn't an indulgence only available to an exclusive or wealthy few. Caring for yourself is a discipline. In America, we often associate self-care with things like luxurious bubble baths, salon appointments, or Egyptian cotton sheets with high thread counts, but self-care is really more practical than that. Self-care is understanding the physical, spiritual, emotional, and mental abilities your life demands and creating enough room in your life to keep up. It's creating enough balance in all four of those areas in order that one doesn't overtake or drown out the rest.

Going to bed at a decent time instead of binge-watching an entire season of a show on Netflix is a form of self-care. Reaching for your Bible when it feels easier to reach for your phone to scroll through Instagram, saying no to some important something because you already have enough *important* on your plate right now—these are self-care too. In the words of my friend Beth, "Self-care isn't about overindulgence or gluttony. It is simply caring enough to treat yourself as Friend instead of Foe."[4]

> Self-care is understanding the physical, spiritual, emotional, and mental abilities your life demands and creating enough room in your life to keep up.

Critics of self-care like to draw attention to the fact that Christ called us to lay down our lives in service, carry our cross, and follow Jesus' example of sacrifice. While all of that is true and it is important that we give grace to others, we need grace also. Perhaps the real problem isn't the idea of self-care, but the word itself. Anything that starts with *self* feels selfish.

As women, we often struggle to take care of ourselves because we struggle to see our own worth. We give great consideration to the needs of others, and rightfully so. But our needs are equally as significant. We matter too. In Christ, belonging has become our birthright.

I have a sneaking suspicion that Jesus never struggled with imposter syndrome. He didn't clamor for the world's approval or suffer from a disease to please. He knew who He was. He knew His value and worth. He had no reason to doubt His identity or feel disapproval because He trusted the "Well done" that mattered most.

When God called Jesus His Beloved Son at the Jordan River, He did so out of unconditional love. Jesus hadn't done anything yet to deserve such love. His identity was as Son, nothing more. He didn't have to earn that approval. It was His by Sonship. As a Christian, you too are beloved by the Father. Your merit is not wrapped up in your ability or your works. You are beloved because you are an heir in Christ—no strings, no striving. God did not choose you because there was no one else better. He chose you on purpose (Eph. 1:4). For that reason alone, you deserve care. The following are a few ways you can provide for your own well-being.

Be in God's Word. Before you reach for that *New York Times* bestselling self-help book to reclaim your identity and purpose, know this: self-help is not the same as self-care. The self-help industry is a billion-dollar boon dedicated to quick-fix, formulaic programs for curing what ails you and improving your life. While *self-help* promises to nurture a better version of the right-now you, Jesus offers total transformation—a brand-new you from the inside out.

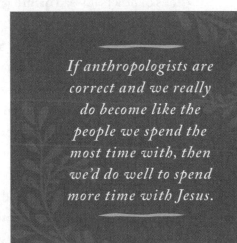

If anthropologists are correct and we really do become like the people we spend the most time with, then we'd do well to spend more time with Jesus.

What if instead of grabbing that self-help book, you and I grabbed our Bibles? What if we stopped preaching to ourselves and actually started listening to the truths God has already given us in His Word? Belief will always determine behavior. So, when we know more about Him by digging deeply into Scripture, we know more about who we are meant to be. His life then becomes the template for ours and we can walk in the freedom that is ours by sonship. If anthropologists are correct and we really do become like the people we spend the most time with, then we'd do well to spend more time with Jesus. To truly take care of ourselves, we need to be in God's Word, memorizing and meditating on the refreshing truth of the gospel, allowing it to make us look more like Christ than simply a better version of ourselves.

Limit the voices. What emotions seem to keep weighing you down? Regret, fear, anxiety, bitterness? Begin to pay attention to the impetus behind that soul clutter. When do you see these feelings begin to surface? If you're anything like me, you notice them most often when you've spent far too much time with a horizontal focus, giving in to social pressures or the unhealthy expectations of others instead of lifting your eyes to Jesus and His callings and claims on your days.

The world offers no shortage of opinions, but not every message is worth your time. When you feel overwhelmed, unworthy, or shamed, begin to limit the voices of influence in your life. This might seem counterintuitive to what God has instructed in places like Proverbs 11:14 that reinforce the practice of having an abundance of counselors. Here's the thing: you get to decide which voices to listen to. If you're not careful to choose wisely, you'll find that too many mentors can lead to mixed messages. Be choosy. It's not enough to have a large number of counselors; make sure that their counsel is quality. Make sure they are reinforcing what you know to be true from God's Word and that they are both affirming and admonishing whenever necessary and appropriate.

Whether you realize it or not, every message you allow in has the power to influence your thoughts and decision-making. The

92

books you are reading, the movies you are watching, the people you are following on social media have all been given a megaphone in your life. For better or worse, you've given them a voice with which to saturate and shape your beliefs about you, your home, your community, and even the God who holds it all together. Before scrolling or binge-watching, be absolutely sure you've not left the back door open for the enemy to walk through. His aim will always be destruction. He'll always lead with shame and guilt. *Care* is the very last thing on his mind.

Pick your boundaries. In those moments when it feels like others are getting the final say in your life, when you constantly feel "voluntold" what to do, when you continue to flinch at the opinions of the experts, you have two choices. You have the right to remain silent, allowing God to take charge of what He chooses to take charge of and then letting go of the rest, or, in the words of writer and podcaster Emily P. Freeman, you have the right to pick your absence, to plan your no's.[5] You have the right to make a list of the groups, causes, social media accounts, or nosy neighbors you don't want to hear from, at least for a time, in order to have the emotional, physical, and spiritual room to listen to the ones who feel like a better fit. You have the right to unsubscribe and unfollow. That's not to say you are putting God in the backseat or that you should only ever listen to those who agree with you or who will tell you things you want to hear. It's just that perhaps, for this moment, you're better served by dialing back on the social noise vying for your attention in order to give God and His still, small voice the consideration He deserves. Perhaps for this season, you need clearer boundaries. You need to give some *hygge* to yourself. Just remember that how others respond to your boundary is not your burden to shoulder.

The toughest part of limiting the voices in your life is deciding when you will stay silent and when you'll say no. While I've never discovered a foolproof way to determine which is the best course of action, if the opinions are not congruent with God's Word, the specific plans He has for my life and my home, I give myself full permission to say no without explanation or trepidation. I'm bold with my no's because I've learned the hard way that a weak no is just an invitation to be asked again from a slightly different angle. Saying no ensures that I never allow another voice to speak louder than the voice of the One who matters most.

Plan for you. For years, I was convinced that to be kind to myself, I could not be kind to others, as if my choice had to be one or the other, as if I couldn't do both. So, when forced to choose, I seldom chose myself. As a girl who was always needed and who never really wore "needy" well, I had to learn to make room for *me* in my own life by leaning heavily on the habits of *hygge*.

One of the best pieces of *hyggelig* advice I've ever received came from my mother-in-law, who knew well the emotional and spiritual dangers of heading into the bleak Minnesota winter without the anticipation of a just-for-me activity. Pointing to the survival instincts of her Danish relations who curate many winter-only diversions for themselves, she encouraged me to find a seasonal hobby that would nurture my mind and heart during the months when everything would undoubtedly be swathed in snow and monotony. A *hyggelig* hobby, she said, would not only help me survive the winter, but it would also help reshape my feelings about the season even before it arrives. I'd be able to look forward to that time instead of confronting it with a sense of dread. She wisely urged me to limit my participation of that hobby to the winter and to pick other hobbies to do in other seasons.

In the same way that the fleeting nature of Christmas traditions like singing carols, baking cookies, and decorating a tree forces you to fully appreciate them because you know they can only be enjoyed during a short span of time, *hygge* hobbies, when purpose-fully pinned to certain months or seasons, can help you anticipate those days. As Ecclesiastes 3:1 reads, "For everything there is a season, and a time for every matter under heaven." In this case, *season* isn't just a length of the year marked by weather patterns. In Hebrew, it's *zeman*, or appointed time.[6] It indicates an ordained purpose; something, or more specifically Someone, outside of yourself who determines the time and eternal reason of this mo-ment. You and I can keep wasting time watching the clock, hoping a particular season will pass quickly, or we can embrace every mo-ment, knowing God has an eternal purpose for them all.

Hyggelige hobbies can give your days a sense of rootedness and rhythm. They can tether you to each season so you can ap-proach your life with expectation. The activities don't have to be elaborate. One year, I committed to spending the winter reading through the back catalog of a new-to-me author. I grabbed the books at yard sales and squirreled them away until late November, which I'd determined was the perfect month to finally crack them open. Another year my teenage daughter and I made a list of clas-sic black-and-white movies we wanted to watch together during the dismal midwinter months.

Lately, I've been taking online violin lessons. At forty-one years old, I'm probably the oldest person ever to screech out "Twinkle, Twinkle, Little Star" with a bow. No matter. My goal isn't to be the next member of the philharmonic; it's to make room in my life for me. It's to preserve my well-being and help me feel like a per-son again. It's to add to my mental, physical, emotional, and even spiritual health in order to grow into a more Christlike version of me. So far, my attempts to play the violin sound as if I'm killing kittens slowly, but every time I play, I'm keeping a commitment to myself. I'm caring enough about me to enjoy the simple pleasures I've planned for during this dark season so I can approach my days with a sense of abundance rather than scarcity.

GROUP CARE

Mark 12:31 reminds us that we are to love our neighbor as ourselves. In other words, the care we give ourselves should never exceed the care we give to others. Generally, Christians easily recognize our responsibility to care for those around us, but it's sometimes difficult to know who to care for and how best to provide care. The needs of this world seem so overwhelming—single mothers struggling to put food on the table, racial oppression caused by generations of systemic injustice, homelessness, sex trafficking, domestic violence, refugees seeking asylum, to name a few. Would the hope and help you or I give even make an impact? How can we use our homes to create a safe haven, a sanctuary of healing and protection when the needs are so great?

While group care is a complicated and nuanced issue, one that can't possibly be cinched up and solved within these pages, there are a few *hyggelige* considerations that can help clear a path toward progress.

Stay for the whole story. How often do we make assumptions about a person or a situation without fully knowing the whole story? Supposing we have all the facts, we give hair-trigger responses as both judge and jury. Case in point, recently while standing in line at the post office, a package balancing precariously against my hip and an alarm going off on my phone, reminding me how late I was for an appointment, I began to grow irritated with the middle-aged woman at the front of the line. She had been standing at the counter since the moment I stepped into the lobby, more than twenty minutes earlier. In that time, the line of disgruntled customers had nearly tripled behind her.

From my vantage point, she looked to be on her cellphone having a conversation with someone when she should have been paying for postage or picking up a package like the rest of us. Murmurs of frustration mounted and morphed into audible expletives, traveling up the line and reaching her ears. We all had places to go and people to see. This woman was a scourge upon our schedules. Ignoring the jeers, she remained steadily in her place. At one point, a handful of people stepped out of the holding pen and headed for the exit, clearly unable or unwilling to wait a minute longer. What could be taking her so long? Why didn't the counter attendant insist the woman get off her phone? Why was she smiling and acting so calmly toward this pokey one? Surely she could see how infuriated the room had become. *This is not your sewing circle, ladies. Save the gossip and witty banter for the next tea party. We've all got lives to live!* I thought, no doubt echoing the sentiments of everyone else in line.

Just when the angry mob was preparing to grab pitchforks to end the small-talk purgatory that held us all hostage, the woman finally turned to leave the counter. A collective gasp rang out from around the room as she tilted her face toward the crowd. She was blind. Apparently, she was trying to register for a post office box and had to have assistance from the other end of

> *We lead with patience and kindness, treating others as image-bearers, drawing them out from behind the bushes of separation and into loving communion with God.*

the cellphone call. Attempting to deflect the whispered taunts she heard from those in line, the counter attendant had shown the blind customer the patience and kindness she deserved.

I'm rightfully remorseful for my treatment of that woman at the post office. I may not have voiced displeasure on my lips, but I certainly shouted it with my body language. Nothing about my behavior toward her or the situation showed her my care or more importantly the care of her Creator. How many times is this same scenario repeated in my days? In yours? How many times do we come to a conclusion before we know all the facts? Before rushing to deliver an indictment of our neighbors, we need to learn to stay for the whole story. We need to lead with patience and kindness, treating others as image-bearers, drawing them out from behind the bushes of separation and into loving communion with God.

When in doubt, dole out dignity. In truth, we can't know the whole of every story every time. People flit in and out of our days quickly. Sometimes we barely have time to look them in the eye, let alone truly see them. But even when we're only given fleeting seconds of connection, we almost always have the opportunity to share the touch of Christ, if not in our actions, certainly in our reactions. First Corinthians 13:7 calls us to consider love. "Love bears all things, believes all things, hopes all things, endures all things." In other words, love assumes the best. It doesn't jump to offense. It doesn't make snap judgments. Love operates with a long leash, giving both grace and the benefit of the doubt. The woman who cuts you off in traffic when you clearly have the right of way—she's hard to love. The teenager who seems incapable of ever getting your fast-food order correctly—he's hard to love too. Small slights such as these often bring about knee-jerk reactions. Instead of leading with 1 Corinthians love, we punctuate the air with a few choice words.

In those harried moments of madness, what if we gave a name to the nameless? What if we offered dignity instead of distrust?

Here's what I mean: When I don't know the person or am not given enough time to get to know the person, as is the case with so many daily interactions, I always try to imagine the stranger in question is someone I know. Before I'm quick to honk my horn at the slow driver who can't seem to decide which lane she wants to be in, I imagine it is Laverne behind the wheel. Laverne is a cherished, gray-haired widow from my church who's mentioned several times how nervous she is behind the wheel since her beloved Earl passed away. Similarly, when I'm tempted to sling out a harsh criticism at the drive-through window attendant when he gives me a #7 instead of the #5 I ordered, I picture my teenage son Reese behind the sandwich counter, trying to learn the ropes on his first day of the job. Before I roll my eyes at the young mom at the grocery store who just handed her screaming toddler a cellphone for amusement, I imagine she is my friend Ellie. Ellie's husband is currently serving his second deployment overseas. It's taking all her energy reserves to play the role of both mom and dad to their three young children. Consequently, she's had to loosen her hold on Plan-A parenting, and rightly so. Picturing the faces of Laverne, Reese, and Ellie has a way of softening my reactions and helps me give others the dignity they deserve regardless of the circumstances.

In our age of high-speed, higher-speed, and highest-speed interaction, online relationships are sometimes the hardest to care for. The anonymity of a screen can build in us a boldness we wouldn't have otherwise. Hiding behind smiling profile pictures, we're quick to serve up hot takes and verbal venom whenever someone has the audacity to disagree with us. But before you give in to your itchy trigger finger and take to your computer with guns blazing, know this: spewing bile on social media will rarely pull anyone over to your side of the aisle. More often than not, it will burn bridges and blast irreparable holes in your relationships.

> Hygge *is about genuine connection.*

With its lack of inflection and expression, even well-intentioned words can come out sideways, causing your sincerity to be misinterpreted.

There is a time and a place for controversial discussions about politics, policies, and personal choices with others. But if you truly care about your neighbor and hope to draw them into the care of Christ, any words of dissent, disapproval, or debate should be saved for face-to-face conversations. *Hygge* is about genuine connection. If you're hoping to connect with others to connect them to the Savior, before starting a clash of words on Facebook or Twitter, ask yourself,

- Will this comment only serve to prove a point, or will it help me build a better relationship?

- Will my words bring honor to this person and this situation, showing that I care, or will they fuel the smoldering embers of societal derision?

Shouting your opinions from a public online platform will not be where you'll affect real change anyway. Sure, you'll gather allies and together you'll be able to stand as moral gatekeepers and digital bullies, double-dog daring anyone to disagree. But no amount of armchair activism will move the needle much, if at all. Transformation will happen best at the dinner table, in the bleachers of your hometown football game, or on the comfy sofa at your next book club meeting. Real change will happen one real conversation at a time.[7]

Determine your banners. The need for care is great. There is no limit to brokenness and separation in this world. So how do you and I even begin to have influence? What parts are we to play? What banners are we to wave? Because the truth is, we cannot care for it all. Don't misunderstand me. I'm not saying we should turn a blind eye or ignore the real pain of others. I'm only saying that knowing and caring are two different things. You can know about a lot of issues, but you cannot care about them all equally. No one's shoulders are wide enough for that. If you do attempt to carry it all, you'll end up physically, emotionally, and financially unable to carry any of it.

In *Liturgy of the Ordinary*, Tish Harrison Warren puts it this way: "When our zealous activism is coupled with a culture of frenzy and grandiosity, the aim of our Christian life can become a list of goals, initiatives, meetings, conferences, and activities that leave us exhausted."[8]

In contrast, Acts 6 reveals a healthy example of social justice. When it was brought to the attention of the disciples that the Greek-speaking Hellenistic widows of the church were not receiving their daily distribution of food like their neighboring Jewish-speaking widows, the twelve men did not stop their ministry of preaching the Word to deliver meals. Instead, they delegated that job. They were not dismissive or indifferent to the need of these widowed church members, but they realized that not every social justice issue was theirs to solve. They knew about the widows' plight but left the care of them to someone else in order to focus their attention on the needs that were theirs to meet. They were quick to conclude that divided allegiances help no one.

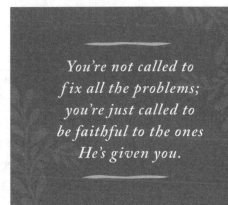

You're not called to fix all the problems; you're just called to be faithful to the ones He's given you.

When you care about everything, nothing actually commands your attention. So don't feel pressured to carry something that is not yours to carry. Trust that God sees and knows every injustice. He hears every groan and cry for help. As He did when the Israelites begged to be released from the clutches of slavery, God will raise up a Moses, someone to serve as ambassador of help and hope amid hardship (Ex. 2:23–25). Sometimes that Moses will be you. Other times, it will be your neighbor. You're not called to fix all the problems; you're just called to be faithful to the ones He's given you.

How will you know which needs are yours to meet? How can you determine where to spend your care? What is the *hygge* that only you can provide? While there's no one hard and fast answer to any of these questions, it's helpful to start paying attention to the overlooked and underserved people God has set right in front of you. Then listen to the Spirit's stirrings. What causes, organizations, or people groups capture your attention? Which ones prick at your own pain? Which have a need you can physically, financially, and prayerfully meet? Think about your abilities, skills, and talents. Think about your passions and personal experiences. Think about your social capital—the people you know and the connections you have made. Where do these intersect? Who or what would most benefit from the earthly assets God has given you?

Like the Danes, whose care for Creation grows through their time investment in nature, your care for the people or policy God brings to you will grow when you pay more attention to it. Your investment of time, energy, and talent will point your heart in the right direction. Once you determine the answer, put your hand to the work and do it with laser focus. Be the person you wish others would be for you. Bring justice, love mercy, and walk humbly (Micah 6:8). These three are what the Lord requires of you.

Remember the aim. Social justice is not limited to Christianity.

The world sometimes serves with compassion very well. There's no end to programs, relief aid, and non-profit entities. But compassion and love are not the same. True love starts and ends with Jesus. As Christians, we have an opportunity to offer the difference. We get to lead the lost and hurting ones to the cross, their only true source of help and healing. In our attempts to fix the world's problems, let's not forget our aim. Jesus came at a hostile political time too, one fraught with injustice, inequality, and oppression. But His focus wasn't to make social change. Justice was a natural side effect of His ministry, but it was not the main goal. Jesus was about His Father's business, which was to bring about salvation. Let's not provide social justice for social justice's sake. Let's be kingdom-minded people who love because He first loved us.

Like most people, I'm passionate about many things—literacy, global poverty, the treatment of children, and Thin Mint Oreos— but none of these should ever transcend my highest priority, Jesus. One day, the world will experience the shalom-peace we've all been longing for since the Garden, on that day when the lion will lay down with the lamb. Then there will be no more need for self-care or group care. For those who are in Christ, well-being will be fully restored. Until that time, may you and I follow His example by caring for ourselves, not selfishly or indulgently, but in a way that enables us to care for others. May we also remember to fight the right battles. That doesn't mean we can't advocate for worthy causes and give voice to policies that need platforms. But we must remember this: while we can't always change what happens in the White House, we can change what happens in *our* house. With the help of *hygge*, we can give our best words and the greatest part of our attention to the one cause that matters most and encourage others to do the same. At the end of our lives, may we be known best for this one simple fight song: Jesus saves, making all things well!

———— CONSIDERING WELL-BEING ————

1. How are you redefining *self-care*?

2. Out of the four areas of self-care mentioned (being in God's Word, limiting the voices, picking your boundaries, and planning for you), which one do you most struggle with and why?

3. Recall a time when you were quick to make assumptions about a person or situation or a time when someone was quick to make assumptions about you. What helped clarify the situation?

4. Whose name can you give to the nameless in order that you can dole out dignity in the middle of a split-second frustration? Begin to brainstorm actual people you know who might make good stand-ins for the next hard-to-love stranger who crosses your path.

5. What are two issues or causes you feel passionate about, feel gifted in, have experience with? How can you provide care to the group of people, the place, or the policy represented?

6. What is one issue you are excited to see others promoting and working toward but that does not garner the same sense of passion in you?

—— TASTE AND SEE ——

- Ephesians 5:29–30
- Hebrews 4:14–16
- Romans 12:1–2
- James 1:27
- Isaiah 1:17
- Zechariah 7:9–10
- Matthew 25:35–36

—— A PRAYER FOR WELL-BEING ——

Yahweh, it is only through connection with You that I can truly know how to give and receive care. You desire a personal relationship with Your image-bearers. Draw me out from behind the bushes of shame and isolation and into communion. Show me when I'm distanced from You. Help me to know how best to care for myself physically, emotionally, mentally, and spiritually so I can be fully able to care for others. Reveal to me what banners I am to wave on Your behalf. Help me to bring the hope of Your Son to the people, places, and policies You've put in front of me so I can contribute to true and lasting justice. Amen.

CHAPTER FOUR

ATMOSPHERE

We shape our buildings and afterwards our buildings shape us.

WINSTON CHURCHILL

W hen making the first home, God did not build, model, or manufacture. He did not assemble or construct. In the beginning, God created. Out of nothing, God made something—but not just *any* something. If *something* was His intention, He would have stopped when His design seemed efficient and serviceable. His brush would have splashed *repetitive* and *dull* onto the canvas, making that first home look sterile and uninspiring. For Creator God, the bare minimum was not the goal of His creativity. But then again, neither was beauty alone. He knew the first home would need both form *and* function.

Theologians point to the meticulous inventory of Genesis to prove that God's Garden home was ordered and well-managed. It had purpose. But what they sometimes fail to mention is that it

> *Theologians point to the meticulous inventory of Genesis to prove that God's Garden home was ordered and well-managed. It had purpose. But what they sometimes fail to mention is that it was also extravagant and enjoyable. It was pretty.*

was also extravagant and enjoyable. It was pretty. From the melodious strains of the songbirds that served no real purpose other than to delight those who would hear them, to the galaxies flung so far they would never be known or seen by anyone but Him, God splurged when He made home. He decorated with all five senses in mind—touch, smell, sight, sound, and even taste. Never in the habit of good-enoughing, He included all His favorites, working until everything was good. Nothing was wasted or wasteful.

In Latin, *create* is translated *creo,* which means to beget or give birth.[1] The Garden God created was not just a place for life but also for living. Later, when God placed humanity there, He charged Adam to "dress it" and "keep it" (Gen. 2:15 KJV). In other words, the new homemakers were to mimic the lavish creativity displayed by their Creator, nurturing a home atmosphere that would lead to life, a home that had both form and function. They were to make spaces that were purposeful, but also pretty.

THE ATMOSPHERE OF JESUS

Jesus obeyed this dress-it-and-keep-it charge when He walked the earth. He naturally reflected the creativity of Garden-like life, drawing humanity out of the dark and into the light in lavish and beautiful ways. As in Creator mode, Jesus gave His very best, sparing

nothing. Granted, apart from His boyhood home, "the Son of Man [had] nowhere to lay his head" (Luke 9:58). For most of His adult life, Jesus was homeless. Nevertheless, Jesus showed us the way to shape a home atmosphere by decorating His days with the kind of creativity that would lead to life.

An atmosphere of humility. Leaving the comforts of heaven, Christ draped Himself in humility: "Who, though he was in the form of God, did not count equality with God a thing to be grasped, but emptied himself, by taking the form of a servant, being born in the likeness of men. And being found in human form, he humbled himself by becoming obedient to the point of death, even death on a cross" (Phil. 2:6–8). He was born into obscurity and later died the agonizing and shameful death of a criminal. But even the cross doesn't paint a completed picture of His humble posture. From His first day to His last, humility found its way into every crack and cranny of His life.

When the crowds rushed upon Him to declare Him as King, humility urged Him to refuse an earthly title of nobility (John 6:15). When He could've received the honor and credit due Him after the miraculous healing of a leper, humility demanded He maintain discretion and anonymity (Mark 1:44–45). When cultural custom dictated that someone wash the dung-covered feet of the weary-worn disciples, humility propelled Him to volunteer (John 13:1–7). Even now, as He sits at the right hand of the Father, humility compels Him to identify with us—to call us His siblings (Heb. 2:11).

An atmosphere of authenticity. When Jesus wore humanity, He was open and available, giving His trusted disciples an intimate glimpse at both His trials and triumphs. Leading with vulnerability, He accessorized Himself with authenticity and welcomed His followers to do the same. As King of kings, Jesus didn't have to let anyone in on His plans and kingdom work. Like most powerful leaders, He could have kept all His cards close to the chest, but He didn't. He was honest about what would happen in this life and in the life to come—the future and forever home. "No longer do I call you servants, for the servant does not know what the master is doing; but I have called you friends, for all that I have heard from my Father I have made known to you," He said (John 15:15). Jesus clearly knew what psychologists are only now discovering: secrecy is one sure path to shame and isolation.[2] He wanted something better for us. He wanted everyone to know Him and be fully known by Him so that we might form sincere relationships with Him and with each other.

An atmosphere of provision. Again and again, Jesus showed that He was not only Maker but Multiplier, pouring out the same something-from-nothing creativity displayed in the Garden. Throughout the New Testament, you'll find examples of how He showed up in the middle of less and provided abundantly more. When no one else thought to pack a lunch, He multiplied some loaves. When water was all that was left, He provided wine. When the nets were empty, He filled them. When hands withered, He healed them. When death came knocking, He brought new life. Less became more. His power was made perfect right there in the middle of so much weakness.

At one point, He used the beauty of Creation to display God's provisional care to weak and worn-out people: "Consider the lilies of the field, how they grow: they neither toil nor spin, yet I tell you, even Solomon in all his glory was not arrayed like one of these. But if God so clothes the grass of the field, which today is alive and tomorrow is thrown into the oven, will he not much more clothe you, O you of little faith? Therefore do not be anxious, saying, 'What shall we eat?' or 'What shall we drink?' or 'What shall we wear?'" (Matt. 6:28–31). Jesus never disappointed or left any hands empty. He provided.

An atmosphere of growth. Jesus' earthly responsibilities included many things: teaching, healing, modeling, discipling. But all these different mantles of ministry had one aim: to draw people toward growth—toward an abundant life in Him. He admonished their sin, releasing them from the bondage of slavery and separation. He encouraged people in their gifts, empowering them to act. He inspired them toward a shared vision, inviting them into service with Him. And He challenged them to outdo one another in their love for others, ensuring that His work would continue long after, "It is finished." The atmosphere of growth He created guaranteed that the original purpose of the first Garden home—life—could be restored to continue forever.

The atmosphere Jesus created with His life was simple, never flashy, never overwhelming. It was basic but beautiful, purposeful and pretty. If you and I are to use our homes to help others feel more at home with Him, we must consider how to create inviting spaces of Christlike humility, authenticity, provision, and growth. Perhaps *hygge* with its unassuming, informal design aesthetic can do a bit of the heavy lifting for us.

HYGGE ATMOSPHERE

Americans often describe Danish style as minimalistic, but that word doesn't really paint an accurate picture of the Danes or their homes. It's probably more appropriate to call their design aesthetic *meaningfulistic*. *Hygge* unintentionally recognizes what Multiplier Jesus displayed all those years ago: that *more* can be found by way of *less*. When outfitting their homes, the Danes quiet their spaces, avoiding the urge to fill a room with trends and momentary passions. Instead, they decorate with clean lines and muted colors. Owning less helps them fully appreciate what they do own even more.[3]

Because they tend to spend quite a bit of time indoors, especially in the winter, they don't mind making long-term investments in furniture in order to buy something that will last. They choose beautiful yet functional, quality over quantity. To our American standards, a Danish home might feel sparse. Perhaps that's because we tend to only think of atmosphere in terms of decor—things we can see. Art on the wall, farmhouse style knick-knacks on the shelves, a stack of photography books collecting dust on the coffee table—this is the stuff of American coziness. Danish design, however, better mirrors a Garden-like atmosphere, appealing to all five senses. The crackling of a fire creates a mood. Comfy chairs draped with fleece blankets caress a space with warmth and comfort. Open windows, hand-crafted wooden accents, and pots of flowering greenery welcome the scents and Garden-like atmosphere indoors. A mug of something hot and delicious creates a finishing touch that says, "Sit and stay awhile." Danes give their attention to creating a home that doesn't just look good but also *feels* good.

Light always seems to get the last word in Danish design. Due to its geographical position in the northern hemisphere, Denmark experiences very few daylight hours during the winter months. Some days, the sun only shows itself for seven hours. Candles are their simple solution, making Denmark the country that burns the most candles per year in the entire world. *Lavende lys,* or "living light" as they are called, not only provide necessary illumination but also a gentle ambiance that can't be replicated by an electric lightbulb. Candles are "instant *hygge,*" bringing light into the dark.[4]

In Denmark, window treatments are left open even at night,

allowing passersby to see the candles and the life happening inside, giving everyone in the community a sense of security and connectedness. When Danes see candles flickering through windowpanes, they know someone is there. They know they're not alone. This simple feeling of community provides a sense of safety.

HOUSE BEAUTIFUL

If a *hyggelig* atmosphere reveals anything about design, it's that while decor does influence mood, there's so much more to creating a life-giving home than a pricy ottoman and decorative wall art. Likewise, the life of Christ shows us that a home should provide an atmosphere where heavy-hearted people can unleash their burdens, find refuge, and be fully fueled and supported so they can go back out into the fray and do God's work in the world. *Home* should be safe *hygge*. Unfortunately, some homes can leave a person feeling ragged, desperate, and destitute, no matter how crowded, costly, or creatively decorated.

In an age when houses are three times larger on average than they were just sixty years ago, we've forgotten what it feels like to be at home in our homes. "Instead of being the epicenter for the cultivation of family life, relationships, productivity, and fruitful service, home has become the place where the equipment (cleats, lunch boxes, backpacks, electronic devices) is stored for the many activities that happen outside the walls of our homes," writes author and speaker Nancy DeMoss Wolgemuth.[5]

Nowadays we have more room to roam inside our houses, but we'd rather be anywhere else. Home has become more about where we get our mail than about where we dwell together. We've forgotten, or perhaps have never learned, how to be cocreators with God, making Garden-like atmospheres that are not just pretty but also purposeful, homes that bring light into dark places—making life and giving life.

An atmosphere of beauty. I used to think spending time, money, and energy to make a home look pretty was careless or, at the very least, evidence of privilege and extravagant spending. After all, wouldn't those resources be better distributed to the least of these? How can you or I possibly justify the cost of wallpaper when 150 million people in the world will fall asleep tonight without the shelter that a plain wall can provide? Both are fair questions and ones that should influence our design decisions, but we'd also do well to remember that beauty was God's idea. "He has made everything beautiful in its time," Ecclesiastes 3:11 reads. Creator God made that first home enjoyable to look at. He gave it both form and function. Both are equally important. It's always worth asking, however, "What is my beautiful space pointing to? What does it reflect about my life to others?"

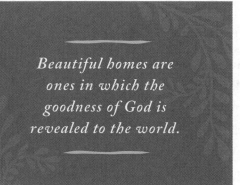

Beautiful homes are ones in which the goodness of God is revealed to the world.

Beautiful homes are ones in which the goodness of God is revealed to the world. Like the Garden, they display the creativity and comfort of the Godhead. They are not perfect homes, mind you, but rather simple spaces designed to make anyone and everyone who enters feel perfectly at home. When purchasing furniture and decor that would make your spaces more appealing, be sure to choose items that would reflect the atmosphere Christ demonstrated. Will that couch, those dining room chairs, that collection of handmade pottery help people walk more humbly in your home, or will they breed a sense of unhealthy pride and vanity? Will their placement within the room encourage authenticity and connection, or will they enable unhealthy seclusion and isolation? Do your design choices provide for the physical, emotional, and spiritual needs of those who spend time in your home, or are they so formal or sterile they make others feel awkward, edgy, or even unwelcome? Will any of your decor allow people to grow in godliness and flourish in the talents and abilities God has given them, or have you inadvertently allowed the form of your rooms to come at the cost of their functionality?

Currently, I have two tables in my dining room. One of them is decent-ish. It's sturdy, matches our boho style, and seats enough people to warrant its coveted spot in the center of the room. The other is weak and well-worn. It sits off to the side, leans at a wonky angle, and bears the scars of two decades of crafts, science projects, game nights, amateur dog grooming attempts, biology dissections, and countless other random acts of big-family madness. (I'll spare you the specifics. You're welcome.) The poor thing looks like it's been on the losing side of a street fight. While not exactly a trend I expect to find in *Better Homes and Gardens* any time soon, a two-table dining room is the *hygge* my home needs. It quietly whispers to my people, "I don't just want you to live here; I want you to find life here."

Don't forget to pay attention to what guests might see when they walk into your house. If you truly want your home to be an inclusive space where anyone and everyone might shelter in the sanctuary of the Savior, your atmosphere can't just be *pretty*. Like in the Garden, it also has to have purpose. As you're able, plan ahead for the needs of others, especially those in a different season of life from yours—the single neighbor, the widower, the mother of small children, the person with special needs. A small bucket of toddler toys, an inflatable mattress with an extra set of sheets, a basket stocked with travel-sized toiletries, a new pair of slippers, even a collapsible wheelchair ramp—all of these can be stashed in a closet and pulled out whenever needed in order to welcome others well. Remember, one great start to helping people to feel at home with the gospel is to make them feel at home in your home.

An atmosphere of order. Denmark is a just society that encourages common sense, not excess. In their less-is-more lifestyle, Danes understand there is no beauty without order. As you can imagine, their homes are shockingly clean and uncluttered. If reading that makes you flinch, please know that *hygge* doesn't demand spotless living. It just recognizes that a chaotic home puts people on edge and creates emotional disarray. *Hygge* helps you strike a healthy balance, motivating you to put forth enough time and effort to show those who cross your threshold that their presence matters to you but doesn't require you to lay a photo filter over your life. I know from personal experience that cleaning a house with little ones (or a sloppy roommate) underfoot is a lot like brushing your teeth while eating Oreos. But that's exactly why *hyggelig* living is so helpful. The Danes own less stuff, making it easier to have a clean-ish house, no matter how many toddlers are in tow.

Perhaps the notion of purging your house seems a bit counterintuitive to creating a sanctuary where everyone feels completely at rest, especially since I also just suggested you look for gently used baby equipment and extra bedding to stash away for potential guests. Remember, owning "stuff" is not a bad thing as long as there's purpose to the "stuff" that you own. So often, when we purchase something, we only think about the cost of buying it. But what about the cost of owning it? When we drag another new-to-us plastic something home, we're always faced with the task of finding a spot on our already crowded shelves for it. We have to dust it every few weeks, shell out our real cash money to maintain it, expend lots of energy watering it, winding it, programming, and reprogramming it. Before we know it, managing our stuff becomes a part-time job. No wonder science shows that our cortisol levels—the hormone connected with stress response—increases when we are faced with cluttered rooms and piles of excess.[6]

Don't be afraid to get rid of that ceramic owl that your husband's great aunt gave you years ago or feel pressured into buying another set of seasonal hand towels simply because they are on sale. That's not to say that you can't keep items for their sentimental value alone or that you should never snag something now while it's deeply discounted so you can eventually use it later. Go ahead, but count the amount of life it will cost you in the long run. It means that you're not saving your nice things for a rainy day, but instead, as humorist Erma Bombeck wrote in a 1979 essay, you have "burnt the pink candle that was sculptured like a rose before it melted in storage."[7] *Hygge* gives you full permission to light the candle, use the good dishes, and wear the expensive perfume because it recognizes that now is always the right time for simple pleasures. Use it, or get rid of it.

> Hygge *gives you full permission to light the candle, use the good dishes, and wear the expensive perfume because it recognizes that now is always the right time for simple pleasures. Use it, or get rid of it.*

Make no mistake, *hyggelig* design doesn't demand scarcity; it simply acknowledges that there's more to beautiful design than what will entice your eyes. This *meaningfulist* lifestyle is especially helpful during certain seasons of the year when we're tempted to overdecorate. Instead of storing dozens of bins of holiday decor in your basement, packing, unpacking, and repacking them each and every year, try achieving the same amount of ambiance and memory-making by incorporating different smells, sounds, tastes, and textures into your space. This kind of perennial decorating will help you step into the change slowly and thoughtfully, lingering in the loveliness of each season before being forced into the next.

Hyggelige homes recognize that nature naturally reflects the season. Take a simple walk around the block collecting natural elements like wildflowers, budding branches, pinecones—any bit of nature that can be gathered in a vase and set on a tabletop. God's design is always seasonally appropriate. What's more, according to the American Society for Horticulture Science, plants have therapeutic, life-giving benefits. Their recent findings revealed that surgical patients experienced lower blood pressure as well as lower rates of pain, anxiety, and fatigue when flowers were brought into their recovery rooms.[8] So if you're going to fill your space with seasonal somethings, do as the Danes and fill it with nature. The moment the flowers begin to wilt or the leaves start to turn brittle, toss them all out and start again. In that way, you'll be inviting the outside in, recreating the atmosphere of the Garden with both sights and smells.

When nature clippings are not an option, try defusing some seasonally specific essential oil blends to recreate natural smells and set the mood. Smell is a powerful force that transports a person in time, connecting memories like no other sense. By using the same blends from year to year, you will be cultivating a sense of cozy nostalgia without having to add another knickknack to your home.

Some of my current favorite seasonal blends include:

- *Spring*: 2 drops chamomile, 2 drops lavender, 2 drops geranium

- *Summer*: 2 drops rosemary, 1 drop lavender, 2 drops sweet orange

- *Fall*: 5 drops clove, 1 drop orange, 1 drop cedarwood

- *Winter*: 3 drops balsam fir, 3 drops black spruce, 1 drop cedarwood, 1 drop juniper

Playlists are another great option for creating seasonal ambiance in your home. Cull a list of your favorite songs that represent certain holidays or special events to add style to your space without adding extra clutter. Compile these on your preferred music app and play them on repeat whenever needed, composing a comforting soundtrack to your days.

Last, don't forget to add light to your *hyggelig* home. Natural light is best, of course. In the spring and summer months, open your curtains and crack a window or two. Not only will you be draping your rooms in vitamin D and the serotonin necessary to keep calm, fight depression, and strengthen your immune system, you'll also be welcoming the sights, sounds, and smells of your neighborhood and local culture into your home. Others will feel more at ease with you when you've found ways to feel more at ease with them. In the fall and winter months, when daylight hours are few, start a fire or light a candle. Warm accent lighting forces slowness and can turn any moment of chaos into a special and unhurried time. Not surprisingly, the Latin word for *hearth* and *fireplace* is *focus*.[9] The soft, crackling flames of a candle or log fire will compel you to stop, take notice, and focus your attention on the present moment and the people sharing it with you.

To the Danes, light offers a sense of security as it illuminates what would otherwise be dark as well as a feeling of community, of the personal presence of neighbors. When light extends beyond the walls and windows of a home, it acts as a beacon of welcome, compelling others to gather near. In that way, the physical lights of your home will be like the luminaries of medieval prayer chapels, helping lost and weary ones find the Light of the World through your front door.

An atmosphere of faith. Every interior design decision starts with a focal point, something that captures attention and draws the eye to look more closely. It's usually a showpiece that encourages curiosity and conversation. That vintage clawfoot tub you've installed in your guest bathroom might garner a few compliments from your mother-in-law and that giant bamboo palm you've crammed in your entryway might capture the attention of your dog walker, but will either compel others to see Christ in your home? Have you made room for the presence of His Spirit within your daily culture, not just on your shelves but in your time and attention in order to make Him the focal point that people can't help but notice?

> *No amount of sloppy agape will do. We must be fully committed to genuine love—love for God and love for others.*

Merely displaying "Christian" wall art does not mean you have a life in line with the life of Christ. If you and I are to create spaces where the Holy Spirit feels welcome and wanted, we must do more than just plunk down a placard in His honor. We must be vigilant to stand guard against the devil, removing anything that would lead to temptation. We must be ruthless and persistent in prayer, calling upon God to help us eliminate sinful attitudes and behaviors we see in our lives. No amount of sloppy *agape* will do. We must be fully committed to genuine love—love for God and love for others.

In addition, if we are to leave room for Christ in our homes, we can't continue to make decisions based solely upon whatever will bring us happiness, comfort, ease, wealth, position, or pleasure. Instead, we need to begin filtering everything through Philippians 4:8, setting our minds on whatever is true, honorable, just, pure, lovely, commendable, excellent, and worthy of praise. From the movies we watch to the songs we listen to, from the money we spend to the activities that command our best attention—every *yes* and *no* we give with our time, talent, and budget should declare that Christ is an unseen but ever-present participant in the culture of our home. Our home atmosphere should reflect the holiness of the Spirit who dwells there.

As Christians living in a time when Christ often comes with a hefty price tag—when there's no limit to how faith can be packaged, commercialized, and peddled like a pyramid scheme, we can become somewhat lazy in our efforts to know the doctrines and principles of the faith we say we prescribe to. We passively consume the verse-of-the-day from that app we downloaded last New Year's and give a quick "heart" on Instagram to the Christian influencer whose daily flat lay or letter board contains a pithy quote that vaguely sounds like something Jesus would have said.

We pop spiritual vitamins because they are easy and don't require any real work or change of consumption from us. We're quite fond of the Bible, but statistics show we're mostly not actually reading it. Like the child who refuses to eat anything but chicken nuggets and potato chips, we're starving ourselves spiritually, depriving our souls of the nourishment they need to thrive.

> *Where we live is not nearly as important as how we live.*

Even though there is at least one Bible in nine out of ten American homes, the people who live there are wasting away in a spiritual famine.[10] We're biblically illiterate, and it shows.

In our efforts to create beautiful homes, let's be women who know Him well, embellishing our days with the time-honored spiritual disciplines that have developed, grown, and strengthened the spiritual lives and homes of women down through the ages. Where we live is not nearly as important as how we live. Let's spend time meditating on and memorizing Scripture, recalling God's faithfulness to His people. Let's be dedicated to prayer and fasting, welcoming a deeper intimacy with Him and preserving our faith from the effects of a decaying culture. Let's have a teachable attitude, dedicated to developing an everyday theology and a working vocabulary of key terms, ideas, and doctrines of Scripture.

Please don't see these basic Christian disciplines as a list of mandatory spiritual checkboxes and to-do lists. Your salvation is secure through grace alone by faith alone in Christ alone. Full stop. Instead, I hope you view them as an invitation to know God and His Word more in order that you might make Him more known to the world. Interestingly enough, any time *create* is used in relationship to Creation and the first Garden home, it's always preceded by the name of God. A home atmosphere is nothing without Him. Be in the Word, and make the Lord your focal point.

To make a life-giving atmosphere, one that displays the humility, authenticity, and provision of Christ and encourages others to grow in faith, we need to design spaces that are not just pretty but also purposeful. Our homes don't need to be flashy or overfilled. *Hygge*, with its basic but beautiful aesthetic, can help us create a place where people live, but where they also find life.

——— CONSIDERING ATMOSPHERE ———

1. Which of the two parts of a *hyggelig* atmosphere do you feel needs your best attention? Which one have you been struggling to nurture in your home: purpose or pretty?

2. When you walk into your home, what is the first thing that you notice about the space? Would guests give the same answer if asked this question about your home?

3. Of the four atmospheres that Jesus nurtured, which do you feel are already present within your home? Which one could use some more focused attention?

4. What can you add, or perhaps subtract, from your space to better appeal to all five senses?

5. Which seasons of life are most represented in your furniture selection and home decor? Which ones are missing? Make a list of specific items that you can add to your space to make both younger and older guests feel more welcome.

6. What item have you been saving for *someday* that could be put to good use *today*?

7. If a stranger were to walk into your home right now, would they sense the presence of Christ? Why or why not? What about your home shows is a place where the Spirit is a welcomed, where He is an unseen participant in the daily atmosphere?

TASTE AND SEE

- Isaiah 40:8
- Proverbs 24:3–4
- Matthew 6:19–20
- Psalm 127:1
- Proverbs 14:1

A PRAYER FOR ATMOSPHERE

Creator God, You have given me this space to dress and keep. Don't allow me to get so preoccupied with making my home look pretty that I lose sight of its eternal purpose. May it be a place where I can walk humbly before You and live authentically before others. Show me how I can best steward my belongings to provide for the emotional, physical, mental, and spiritual needs of those You bring to my door. I invite Your Spirit into this space. Help me know You more each day so that I might make You better known to the world. Amen.

COMFORT

Where God is in your loss matters more to a doubting
and cynical world than where God is in your plenty.

ROSARIA BUTTERFIELD

W hen inspiring His scribe to write the story of that first home, God skipped over flamboyant and colorful names like *Paradise, Utopia,* or *Heaven on Earth.* Instead, He christened it with the more subtle monikers of *Garden* and *Eden.* Some might argue that name choice is merely semantics, and that a rose by any other name would smell as sweet, but there was purpose in His pick. God never spends one syllable wastefully.

Garden, or *gan* as it's written in Hebrew, means enclosure and is loosely associated with the root word *ganan,* which means to defend, cover, or surround—it symbolizes protection.[1] *Eden,* on the other hand, means pleasure.[2] Two names that seem so wildly conflicting were purposefully penned to describe a home that provided everything that first couple needed most. Like the soft blanket a mother uses to swaddle her baby, wrapping him in the protection and the sweet pleasure of her arms, the Garden home enveloped Adam and Eve in the comfort of God.

Eden was a sanctuary, set apart from all the rest of Creation, an inner sanctum. It was here that humanity would experience the comfort of their Creator. But when sin entered, God's hand of protection was lifted, leaving the pair open and exposed. From that moment on, things would no longer be good. Tears and toil would define their work. Destruction, disease, and death would lurk behind every shadow. All the pleasure of that place would be forfeited to the pain of somewhere else. Where once they had been hedged in, they were now blocked out. They were forced to leave the Garden and all the comfort they had grown comfortable with.

> Even as God's holiness demanded retribution, His kindness promised reconciliation—a return of His comfort, not in a place but in a Person.

THE COMFORT OF JESUS

God could have left it at that; He could have washed His hands of humanity. After all, He had given them every chance to obey, provided them with everything they could possibly have wanted and needed—and in return, they rebelled. They disregarded His simple instructions, defied His authority in their lives, and single-handedly sabotaged their eternal inheritance. The punishment was swift and just. But even as God's holiness demanded retribution, His kindness promised reconciliation—a return of His comfort, not in a place, mind you, but in a Person. "I will put enmity between you and the woman, and between your offspring and her offspring; he shall bruise your head, and you shall bruise his heel," He said (Gen. 3:15), declaring that one day, a Comforter would come and make all things good again.

True to His word, God sent Jesus at just the right time. Suffering under the tyrannical fist of the Romans, the Israelites assumed this Messiah would be a Davidic king who would rule and reign with justice, peace, and prosperity. Jesus could have easily released His friends and neighbors from the oppressive grip of their political enemies, providing them with both protection and pleasure, but He didn't. When He could have filled every belly, mended every bone, given sight to every blind eye, comforted every broken heart, He didn't. His Garden-like restoration came, but when it did, it looked much different from what they were expecting. His work was not to remove the discomfort people felt in this life but to overcome it for all of eternity. What sometimes looked like defeat ended up being a great victory. The turnaround was never immediate, but it was always right on time.

For instance, when Lazarus was sick, Jesus did not rush off to heal. He waited, leaving onlookers to wonder about His lukewarm response. *How could He sit idly by for two days while His beloved friend suffered and died? How could He be so complacent when He had the power to heal? What kind of Comforter would let pain have the last word?* On the other side of the story, we of course know the answer to all those questions. We have the benefit of hindsight. Jesus was not sent to raise one man from the dead but to raise all of humankind to life. Work was happening in their hearts when it seemed like Christ was silent. If the healing had come on Mary's and Martha's timetable, they would have seen their brother's physical resurrection but would have missed their own spiritual one. The waiting period compelled the women to give up on their ability to help. It forced them to relinquish control so that Christ would receive greater glory (John 11:4). The delay ensured that Lazarus was not just dead; He was deader than dead. In accordance with the Jewish custom, by the fourth day, His spirit had left his body and all hope for healing was lost. Arriving on the scene, Jesus wept, comforting Mary and Martha by stepping into their grief. But the purpose of His comfort was never just to dry the tears of hurting ones but to show them compassion with action. With His Father's blessing, Jesus called Lazarus out of the grave, displaying His power and authority over death and growing the faith of many that day.

Later as He hung on the cross, enduring unimaginable pain, Jesus never wavered from His divine call to comfort, not only for those He loved most but for everyone. As He struggled to take a few final breaths, He saw His mother, Mary, standing not far off, sharing in His suffering. Scripture calls her "blessed among women," and yet her life was riddled with disappointment, rejection, and unfathomable loss. She may have been the mother of God's own Son, but she was not exempt from the consequences of that first Garden sin. She spent nine months and, no doubt, many years following her scandalous pregnancy, suffering the contempt and scorn of others. Church tradition asserts that her husband, Joseph, died sometime before Jesus' earthly ministry, leaving her to shoulder the family burdens alone. As the prophets foretold, she was forced to watch as her friends and neighbors duplicitously planned and carried out the gruesome execution of her son. Her life looked anything but blessed to our worldly estimation.

Yet none of Mary's pain was accidental, and none went unnoticed. Christ saw all of it. In His perfect timing, He provided comfort:" When Jesus saw his mother and the disciple whom he loved standing nearby, he said to his mother, 'Woman, behold, your son!'" (John 19:26). Knowing that widows and sonless mothers were easy targets for abuse and neglect, Jesus used some of His last moments to place His mother in John's care, ensuring that she would not only be given physical protection but also the pleasure of familial love. Moments later, He surrendered His life. In doing this, Jesus restored the comfort of the Garden. God's hand of protection was removed from Him and placed on her, sealing her from the punishment of sin. The pain Jesus willingly endured provided Mary the pleasure of dwelling with Him forever in heaven. This comfort came at a high cost; but it was true and lasting, not just for her, but for everyone who would one day put their faith and trust in Him.

Even after her son's ascension into heaven and His promise to go and prepare a place for her, Mary was not naïve enough to think the rest of her days on earth would look any different from before. Bills would stack up on her counter. Neighbors would continue to gossip. An aging body would give way to aches and pains. Trouble would find her because Jesus promised that it would. But Mary would "take heart" and face it all with courage knowing that with His death, Jesus overcame it all (John 16:33). Comfort wouldn't always be instant, but it would come eventually—if not in this life, certainly in the next.

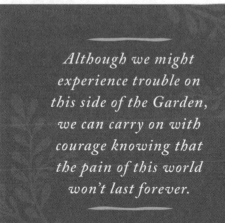

Although we might experience trouble on this side of the Garden, we can carry on with courage knowing that the pain of this world won't last forever.

HYGGE COMFORT

Christ's "Take heart" promise wasn't just for Mary; it was for all of us. It was a reminder that although we might experience trouble on this side of the Garden, we can carry on with courage knowing that the pain of this world won't last forever. Quite unwittingly, the Danish people capture this kind of Christlike courage whenever they *hygger*.

Admittedly, the Danes are not typically overemotional nor prone to dramatic displays. While at first blush their stoicism can make them seem reserved and aloof, their solace is steady and sincere. They don't try to erase pain or even dismiss or belittle it. Pain and shadow are unavoidable this side of the Garden even for the "happiest people on earth." Instead, they find ways to embrace sorrow, knowing that too much sweet will rot the teeth and leave a person with a bellyache. It's the bitter tang of salt that balances the flavor. The Danes recognize that a person can't ever be truly happy if they've never experienced unhappiness. If they are to fully enjoy life, they can't run from calamity.

One particular burden those in Denmark must learn to carry well is winter. The sub-zero temperatures and lightless days of near-tundra living can create a perfect breeding ground for Seasonal Affective Disorder, or SAD as it is more commonly known. Winter is isolating, and it's also unavoidable. To evade the gripping fingers of depression and despair, the Danes cling to the restorative rituals of *hygge*. Often called their language of consolation, *hygge* helps them carry grief and joy at the same time, while not being overcome by either. *Hygge* is comfort in moderation. It is a rational voice that declares, "If you choose not to find joy in the snow, you will have less joy in your life but still have the same amount of snow."

Predictability plays a big role in *hyggelig* comfort. The Danes find safety and pleasure in knowing what was, what is, and what will be. Keepsakes, habits, and routines line their memory with familiarity and emotional warmth, training their behaviors and responses. So, even when it's mind-numbingly cold outside, they can still feel layered in the folds of everyday comforts and habitual affections.

It's *hygge* they feel when they hear a familiar song come on the radio or when they slouch in the encircling arms of a favorite chair. It's *hygge* that drives them to thumb through the tattered, hand-written recipes of a beloved grandmother. *Hygge* compels them to lean into the person sitting next to them during the tense scene of a movie, gently sway their bodies to calm a teething baby, reach for the embrace of a loved one after days or weeks of separation. Like in the Garden, the comfort of *hygge* is almost always connected to their feeling of physical protection and emotional pleasure. It's not that these simple, daily rituals only happen in Denmark. Obviously, they don't. It's just that the Danes have learned to celebrate what the rest of us often fail to see or truly appreciate, and that deliberate mindfulness makes all the difference, especially on a difficult day.

THE MINISTRY OF MISERY

Winter is the most *hyggelig* season in the Danish calendar. When all of creation is wintering and the landscape looks dormant and fallow, the Danes remember that life is still happening just below the surface of the soil. Winter prepares the way for new things to break through. Through our Western eyes, we're quick to call the dirt of this life *filthy* or *ruin*, forgetting that it was by dirt that the Master Potter made us in the Garden all those years ago. It is by dirt and snow that life continues to renew and grow. In praying that God takes away the struggles of this world—the dirt and snow—we're also unwittingly disregarding the comfort that lies on the other side of every discomfort we face.

As Romans 8:17 reminds us, we're not just blessed with the glorious riches of Christ, but also with His suffering. In only tacking "blessing" onto the non-winter seasons of life—the times we experience financial gain, a new job, or good health—we are fracturing the gospel by negating the real and raw truth of God's love for the whole world. We are saying He prefers to place His hand on the wealthy, privileged pew-sitters, not the persecuted church huddled in a hut singing praises together on some foreign soil or the man in a prison cell who just hasn't heard God's still, small voice yet and so he's not yet come to repentance in faith—that there's something about us that is more "blessable" than them. Let's not forget that God loved His Son, and yet Jesus' story still contained a cross. Mary was "blessed among women" and yet she had to witness the brutal death of her firstborn child. Harsh winters, to be sure.

> The true blessing promised in Scripture is always tethered to spiritual prosperity—to our relationship with God and whatever will draw us closer to Him.

If their stories teach us anything it's this: the true blessing promised in Scripture is always tethered to spiritual prosperity—to our relationship with God and whatever will draw us closer to Him. Sometimes in God's love for us, He walks us through the bleakness of winters, not around it. He knows that in our emotional poverty, we will lean harder, cling tighter, trust longer while sitting in pain than in pleasure. Our winters will make us desperate for Him and the comfort only He can provide.

Comfort is a small word, but it begs a big question: When we're stuck in the messy middle of earthly living, how can we point others to the pleasure and protection of Christ? How can we provide comfort when we might be sitting in the discomfort of a winter season ourselves? I've wrestled with this question many times and have always come to the same two conclusions. The first is this: God is in the business of resurrection and can bring life into all our dead and wintery places. And the second? The "making of all things new" is sometimes a slow process. Spring won't *happen* overnight, but it *will be happening* overnight. In the middle of the transformation when our gardens still look and feel more like graveyards, we can be busy doing kingdom work.

Like the Danes who welcome the relentless snow, knowing that whether they embrace it or not, the snow will fall, we can cling to certain restorative rituals in the dark seasons of life. We can implement a few *hyggelige*-like liturgies to help us develop habitual affections in our discomfort.

Pray. Often when we don't know what to do in a difficult season—when we've exhausted all our resources and cashed in all our chips only to find what we hoped to fix in our lives or the lives of others is still broken—we slump our shoulders and whisper under our breath, "Well, I guess all I can do now is pray." Prayer becomes our last resort, a sort of white flag of surrender.

But prayer isn't just telling God your need. After all, He knows about it already. Prayer is releasing that need back to Him. It's anything but surrender. It's the opposite of passivity; it's action. It is handing over our fears, our doubts, our

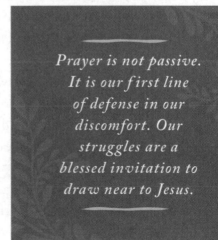

Prayer is not passive. It is our first line of defense in our discomfort. Our struggles are a blessed invitation to draw near to Jesus.

questions. It is calling upon God for wisdom. It's relinquishing our rights, admitting our faults, and placing the control in the hands of the One who can move heaven and earth on our behalf. No, prayer is not passive. It is our first line of defense in our discomfort. Our struggles are a blessed invitation to draw near to Jesus. He can untangle and restore. Whatever you or I cannot account for or solve, the blood of the Lamb will surely cover in our lives. We will never be able to carry some burdens, but God can and will carry it all.

Additionally, prayer is the great unifier of our faith. When Jesus gave us an example of prayer, He used collective pronouns: *us, our,* and *we.* His prayer gathered us all under His comfort. The unity of His prayer continues to collect our tears together. You and I no longer have to go it alone. Bearing one another's burdens is part of the privilege and inheritance of being coheirs with Christ.

Praise. First Thessalonians 5:18 reads, "Give thanks in all circumstances; for this is the will of God in Christ Jesus for you." Being told to be thankful *always* can feel like a gut punch when your situation feels like a wasteland. "What is there to be thankful for?" you might find yourself asking. But notice the verse does not say you have to be thankful *for* all circumstances. Instead, it calls you to be thankful *in* all circumstances. *Hygge* is the bridge that spans the gap between the two. *Hygge* reminds you that although in this season of winter everything feels brittle and barren, without death there would be no life. Joy can come in the mourning. *Hygge* helps us acknowledge our pain and praise together in a perfectly timed duet.

You don't have to be thankful for the hail damage, divorce papers, or bad performance review. You don't have to be thankful for the fire that left you homeless, the illness that's rendered you dependent upon others, the drunk driver who crossed the median at the worst possible moment. God never expects us to be thank-

ful *for* the pain. All He asks is that
we're thankful *in* it—that we lean
into the goodness of Him.

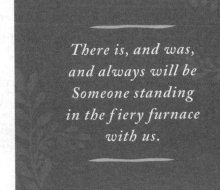

> *There is, and was,
> and always will be
> Someone standing
> in the fiery furnace
> with us.*

Gratitude under painful duress
can feel like a tall order. But the
truth is, an experience, *any* experience, will either bring you toward
God or push you away from Him.
Your belief will determine your behavior, so the choice is up to you.
Bitterness is the byproduct of false
theology and will take root whenever we begin to believe God got
it wrong or that He didn't "show up" whenever and however we
wanted Him to. In the same way the Danes embrace the predictable
nature of *hygge* to ward off the resentment that often follows discomfort, you and I need to remember there is, and was, and always
will be Someone standing in the fiery furnace with us. His presence
can and will provide the protection and pleasure—the comfort—
we need no matter how hot the flames of affliction become.

This is the very restorative ritual the prophet Samuel used to
reorient the hearts of God's people. Like an ominous cloud of destruction, the Philistine army invaded the Israelite land. The people were frozen in fear. Looking beyond what seemed like a big
discomfort in front of him, Samuel set his eyes on his big God.
He drew near. Placing a lamb upon an altar, he cried out to God in
worship. Worship was his warfare. Seeing Samuel's thankfulness *in*
the midst of misery, God threw the Philistine army into confusion,
allowing the men of Israel to utterly destroy them. When the dust
settled, Samuel set up a stone of remembrance, an Ebenezer, to
bear witness to God's care (1 Sam. 7). From that day on, any time
one of the men or women of Israel looked upon that stone, they

remembered how the Lord was faithful to them. Remembrance was a small, intentional act that helped them set their hearts on this truth: if God was faithful *then*, He can be counted on to be faithful *now*.

If you feel battered and bruised, begin to stack Ebenezer stones of remembrance and praise. Begin to take every negative thought captive and replace it with truth by starting each day asking yourself, "How has God been faithful to me in the past? How has He been faithful today?" Write your answers on a stone. Stack these in a jar, then take them out for remembrance as often as you need to. Don't worry, the shine won't wear off from overuse. Raise an Ebenezer to stand as evidence to you and to others of God's goodness that was and is and always will be.

Forgive. As a woman who has been both predator and prey, I know that extending forgiveness is never easy. Some wounds cut too deep. Sometimes the person who did the cutting is still holding the knife. No matter the situation, we don't get an *out* in this. We can't earn immunity here. Those of us who are in Christ are called to forgive in the same way we've been forgiven. Forgiveness is required. Period.

Perhaps that harsh reality feels impossible because the pain is too raw. Maybe the mere mention of the word *forgiveness* makes your blood congeal. I get it. I also find it easier to toss all my losses in some kind of emotional junk drawer, assuming if I can just slam it shut hard enough, all the pain will remain locked up—out of sight, out of mind. Or worse, I underrate and overlook small bruises. "Sturdy up and move on" becomes my rallying cry. But the truth is, pain doesn't have to come by way of a bullet to matter. Even a paper cut can kill you, one tiny drop of blood at a time, if it's not dealt with properly.

The world has painted forgiveness in all the wrong colors, and consequently, we don't always understand or recognize what it means to forgive and be forgiven. Forgiveness is not reciprocity. Sometimes apologies are offered, and sometimes they're not. Forgiveness is not reconciliation. Sometimes relationships are restored, and sometimes the offender refuses to repent, creating further brokenness in the relationship. Forgiveness should happen either way.

"I forgive you" doesn't always come easily to our lips because forgiveness seems like *forgetting* or like letting someone off the hook. But forgiveness is neither of these. It's actually a way to say, "Something evil happened here—something so evil it cost Jesus His very life." Forgiveness gives the offense the gravity it deserves. It cancels a debt and removes the control an offender has over you. In that way, it's a gift you can give to yourself. When you allow the hurts of others to linger too long without your forgiveness, that hurt turns into hate. Hate simmers into bitterness. Bitterness leads to vengeance on your part. Now theirs is not the only sin that needs to be addressed. To garble an ancient Japanese saying, "He who seeks revenge should dig two graves."[3] When left unchecked, your vengeance will destroy a life. Yours. Forgiveness, however, puts justice in the right hands. It gives all the responsibility of retribution to God. You no longer have to bear the burden of someone else's sin. Forgiveness is your one sure path to freedom.

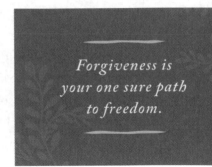

Forgiveness is your one sure path to freedom.

Share. In your misery, be brave enough to tell your story. Share your pain with your family, friends, and neighbors. Don't leave out the embarrassing parts or the painful parts. Although God was not necessarily the author of your pain, in His redemptive way, He can and will use it to allow others to see His faithfulness or to open the door for them to experience the joy of giving, serving, ministering to, and praying for you. It reveals to them a small portion of their kingdom purpose and gives them a chance to exercise their spiritual gifts.

We were made to live in community. The Danish people would call this way of living *omsorg*—the idea of being cared for and provided for.[4] It's the kind of tender *hygge* that comes back at you. Part of being able to minister in your misery is to allow others the opportunity to minister to you. Keeping your pain private denies your friends and family the ability to enjoy *hygge* in their own lives. When you're brave enough to show your scars to others, you declare that both your celebrations and your sufferings belong to the Lord. In doing so, you steward them both well.

Provide. A *hyggelig* mindset is braced by the seasons. It urges you to remember that no matter how bleak the winter, the earth will eventually give way to spring. The snow won't last forever. To everything, there is a season. In other words, that wound won't bleed you dry. A scar will form in time. It might feel like that betrayal, that miscarriage, or that assault created an irreparable chasm in your life, leaving your emotions and perhaps even your body in critical condition. But it hasn't. In time, life will bloom again.

God will never give you protection and pleasure—comfort—that He does not want you to give away to someone else someday. In that way, your pain will have purpose. As 2 Corinthians 1:3–5 says, "Blessed be the God and Father of our Lord Jesus Christ, the Father of mercies and God of all comfort, who comforts us in all our affliction, so that we may be able to comfort those who are in any affliction, with the comfort with which we ourselves are comforted by God. For as we share abundantly in Christ's sufferings, so through Christ we share abundantly in comfort too."

Maybe not today, maybe not tomorrow, but someday your scars will become your credibility, transforming your misery into a ministry.

In full disclosure, comforting others will rarely be convenient. It will often be tempting to turn the channel or look away instead of revisiting the hurt of your past. But remember, a *hyggelig* life compels you to know someone well enough not just to serve them bread, but also to bear their burdens. You don't have to have all the answers. People need *you* to show up before your advice shows up. Sometimes standing in quiet companionship can speak the language of love in powerful volumes. But should you want clear direction for how you can comfort someone in their deepest pain, just think back to the ways that God held your story with care, and then do the same for the stories of others. Don't worry about saying or doing everything perfectly. Just point to the Comforter, remembering that a home centered on God can provide comfort inside even when outside the world is crumbling.

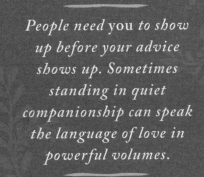

People need you *to show up before your advice shows up. Sometimes standing in quiet companionship can speak the language of love in powerful volumes.*

HURT CAN HELP

When people are in crisis, their most deeply held beliefs about God emerge. Questions come to the surface. Don't be afraid to let others ask them, and don't assume their questions and concerns will lead to unbelief. Every person on earth and throughout history has wrestled with *why*, even Jesus. The important thing is to help others bring those questions to the One who can answer them best. Amid a depraved culture, Habakkuk was brave enough to say, "I keep praying, and yet I don't seem to ever get an answer. Why? There's so much violence, injustice, and pain in this world. Why? I look around and all I see is the wicked prospering. Why?" (Hab. 1:1–4, paraphrased).

As a Christian, you have probably asked those same *why* questions in the middle of your winters. Like Habakkuk, you learned to set those questions next to the character of a God who makes and keeps the promise of bringing good and not harm. Isaiah 51:3 reminds us that He can comfort our "waste places" and turn our wilderness into Eden:

> For the LORD comforts Zion;
>   he comforts all her waste places
> and makes her wilderness like Eden,
>   her desert like the garden of the LORD;
> joy and gladness will be found in her,
>   thanksgiving and the voice of song.

The Lord will comfort His people, using every parched and painful part of our lives to bring about the eternal pleasure of Eden. The sorrows of this world may continue to cause deep heartache for us or our neighbors, but we can't confuse *hurt* with *harm*. In their book *Boundaries,* Drs. Henry Cloud and John Townsend assert, "Things can hurt and not harm us. In fact, they can even be good for us. And things that feel good can be very harmful to us."[5]

Fortunately for us, God knows the difference between hurt and harm and has promised that in His great love for us, we will not be consumed (Lam. 3:22 NIV). On the contrary, according to Revelation 21:5, He is right now—at this very moment—making all things new for you, for me, and for anyone else who has put their faith and trust in Him. God is making spring. *Making* is a present participle verb that implies an action that is currently happening but hasn't come to completion. In other words, the story of your present *hurt* isn't done yet. Don't rush your way through to the resolution, assuming the pain is happening *to* you. Perhaps instead the pain is happening *for* you.

Jesus puts it this way: He is the vine and we are the branches (John 15:5). God, in His great love for us, will trim back and cut away parts of our lives for our good. It might seem counterintuitive to prune a vine to help it grow better fruit, but any vinedresser will tell you that pruning is necessary. It allows him to focus on quality, not quantity. He'll cut off 85–90 percent of the first-year growth and will continue to meticulously prune and shape the vine for two more full seasons until it can produce the kind of choice, mature fruit needed for winemaking.[6] After years of waiting, the vinedresser will begin to see vines laden with plump, luscious grapes. Even then, he must resist the urge to pluck them. Their ripening is not quite done. It will take the bitter cold of the first frost to mature them to the desired sweetness. It will take the beginning of winter. Once picked, the grapes will be crushed under extreme pressure. If the vinedresser were to skip any step of the process—pruning, frosting, or crushing—the fruit would never become what it was intended to be.

Please don't mistake my sincerity in this. I've no intention of disregarding or dismissing your very real pain. I too have experienced a fair share of winters in this life. My childhood was laden with abuse of every conceivable kind. The deep sadness that accompanies death and disease has lingered at the edges of many of my adult days. Although at times I've felt strangled by the struggle, I can now look back and see how much I was formed by it. I can see how God used all of it to produce good fruit in my life. Even when I didn't know Him or didn't recognize His hand, the Lord was moving mountains on my behalf. He's been keeping watch my entire life.

Whether you realize yet or not, God has done the same for you too. Pruning, frosting, and crushing are painful, but they can also mature you to completion if you let them. It sometimes helps to remember that pruning isn't always necessary because of death and disease. Sometimes healthy parts have to get pruned so something bigger and better can have a chance to grow. Admittedly, that truth might not feel very comforting in your broken places. The pain of this present moment might feel too hard for you to care much about the future pleasure and protection you'll enjoy with Christ someday. That's fair. You're allowed to feel that way. Your disappointment, frustration, and even rage do not shock or surprise God. No amount of "Sunday face" is going to hide the truth of your Monday feelings from *El Roi*, the God Who Sees. So be honest about your discomfort. He invites you to. He is the God who bends down to listen, who inclines His ear and wants to hear not only your hallelujahs but also your hurts (Ps. 116:2).

> *As He comforts you, comfort others. In doing so, you'll be declaring to the world that sanctuary is possible.* Hurt *will not win.*

As grace would have it, God is not an apathetic listener. Psalm 56:8 declares that God will faithfully keep count of all your tossing and put your tears in a bottle. He will write them all down in

His book. He will fully restore your brokenness by buying it back with the blood of His Son. He doesn't just cover it, He redeems it. Let this promise be a balm to your wounded and weary heart. If He's measuring your sorrows, that means they are measurable. They won't last forever. There will be an end to them. Because of Christ's "Take heart" message of John 16:33, you can be sure your pain will eventually lead to protection and pleasure. As He comforts you, comfort others. In doing so, you'll be declaring to the world that sanctuary is possible. *Hurt* will not win.

--- CONSIDERING COMFORT ---

1. Which of the two parts of Garden-like comfort feels the most out of reach for you right now—the protection of God or the pleasure of God? Why?

2. What is most discomforting about your life right now?

3. How can you be thankful in that circumstance today? List three to five thoughts of gratitude and worship.

4. Who do you need to forgive today?

5. Recall a time when God was faithful to you in a difficult circumstance. How has He turned that previous misery into ministry in your life? Can you imagine any way you might use this current discomfort for kingdom purposes?

6. Is there someone in your life who could use Christlike comfort from you today? In what ways can you carry their story with care?

--- TASTE AND SEE ---

- Isaiah 41:10
- Deuteronomy 31:8–9
- Psalm 46:1–3
- Psalm 23
- Psalm 121

A PRAYER FOR COMFORT

Comforter, this world is so broken. Death and destruction seek to destroy. In my pain, may I feel Your hand of protection around me. Remind me of the pleasure I have waiting for me in the second Garden of heaven someday. As I wait for that day, show me ways I can use my misery to minister to others in the same way You have kindly ministered to me. Thank You for making all things new in my life. Even in a bitter winter season, may I always recall that You are the God Who was, is, and always will be faithful. Amen.

CHAPTER SIX

CONTENTMENT

"It's snowing still," said Eeyore gloomily.
"So it is."
"And freezing."
"Is it?"
"Yes," said Eeyore. "However . . . we haven't had an earthquake lately."

A. A. MILNE

T he enemy came slinking into that first Garden home, speaking with the accent of death. His message was crafty but uncomplicated: *Did God really say?* These four little words suggested that God got it wrong and His gifts were not still good.

The enemy's short speech was seductive, enticing Eve to shift her perspective and fix her eyes on the greener grasses of sinful superlatives. The good of God's Garden was no longer good enough, she reasoned. She craved something better. Surely, her best life was just one bite away. Her shortsightedness—her inability to see beyond the thing right in front of her—became her undoing. Ignoring the clear instructions of her Creator, she reached for the forbidden fruit, surrendering her right to God's sovereign plan and the inheritance of perfection He had provided. Sin may have been the cause of her death that day, but it came by way of discontentment, a weapon Satan has been wielding on humanity ever since.

THE CONTENTMENT OF JESUS

When the first Adam fell for Satan's temptations, his paradise became a wilderness—a desolate wasteland ruled by self-preservation, self-promotion, and self-sufficiency. He traded the good gifts of God for an unholy trinity of *self*, as 1 John 2:16 puts it: "The desires of the flesh and the desires of the eyes and pride of life." Years later when the Second Adam, Jesus, was led by the Spirit to fast and pray for forty days, the enemy vowed to restore order by turning the wilderness into a paradise if only Jesus would make that same seedy swap.

"Aren't you hungry, Jesus? At your word you can turn these stones into bread," he tempted. "Show the world who you really are. Leap from this pinnacle. The angels will surely catch you. Claim what is rightfully yours, Jesus. Kneel before me now and in exchange, I'll give you all the kingdoms of this world" (Matt. 4:1–11, paraphrased). This was a calculated attack on Christ's contentment. It was the same sneaky appeal that had taken out every other person before Jesus—a promise to fulfill His physical appetites, empower Him spiritually, and advance Him socially. As he did in the Garden with Eve, Satan hoped he could persuade Jesus to shift His perspective and grow discontentment. He served up the shiny fruit of godlike power and wisdom. Yet the Son of Man was not concerned with promoting Himself.

Jesus knew who He was. But more importantly, He knew *whose* He was, and that perspective made all the difference. As the Son of the Most High, Jesus was heir to an inheritance that would never perish, spoil, or fade (1 Peter 1:4). Ironically, during His earthly life, Jesus had little. If placed against the extravagance of American culture, he'd be the guy at the corner with the cardboard sign—the beggar with an empty bowl. But He refused to let His current status or lack of stuff define His

> *Jesus had no reason to make a power play, scratching and clawing for more. He could willingly lay down His life because He knew His Father was the giver of good gifts and would provide all that He needed, not just in life but also in death.*

story. Instead, He continued to express gratefulness for both the position and provision God had given Him. In direct contrast to the temptations of the wilderness, Jesus even gave thanks for the cup of suffering He would face on the cross (Matt. 26:26–27). He had no reason to make a power play, snatching and grabbing for more. He could willingly lay down His life because He knew His Father was the giver of good gifts and would provide all that He needed, not just in life but also in death.

Contrary to what we're often led to believe, the wilderness isn't always a place of ruin and despair. In this case, the wilderness was a place of preparation. After leaving all the comforts of the world to fast and pray in the desert, Jesus appeared to be weak and vulnerable. In reality, He was quite the opposite. His empty arms weren't a sign of defeat; they were a sign of surrender. There in the wilderness, unhindered by the distractions of this life, He was able to focus all His attention on God and God alone.

When the devil appeared, dangling shortcuts to eternal perfection, his temptations proved fruitless. Jesus reached for the Word of God instead. Recalling the passage from Deuteronomy 8 that was given to the children of Israel as they wandered in the wilderness many years before, the Second Adam spoke truth out loud to strengthen His resolve and to provide a proper perspective of His present circumstances. "Man shall not live by bread alone, but by every word that comes from the mouth of God. . . . You shall not put the Lord your God to the test. . . . You shall worship the Lord your God and him only shall you serve" (Matt. 4:4–11). True to form, the Word became a double-edged sword, a battle-ready defense against deadly desires.

HYGGE CONTENTMENT

The Danish people have learned to deflect discontentment. When faced with the temptation to complain about their current circumstances, they remind themselves of what they know to be true. "There's no such thing as bad weather, only bad clothing" is their *hyggelig* mantra. Although certainly not on par with Scripture, this nearly constant refrain in many Scandinavian countries holds some value.

To the casual listener, such a saying sounds like a platitude, a blanket solution to help shore up their emotions for the impending cold. (Not to belabor a point, but for much of the year, the Danes face weather most meteorologists around the world would deem severe, fierce, and even intolerable.) But they speak those words boldly like an anthem, proudly proclaiming their determination to not just endure winter but to enjoy it.

Here in the tundra-ish woods of northern Minnesota, where the wind chill can make the "feels like" temperature dip to −50 degrees

Fahrenheit on some days, *bad weather* feels like a rather generous term. Not surprisingly, it takes a certain strength of character to find joy during the harsh realities of white-out winters.

Severe weather is a relatively easy adversary to face. Lots of layers and sensible shoes are, in fact, surefire weapons for surviving snow and ice. But the truth of that *hyggelig* saying goes deeper than the plummeting thermometer reading. The Danish attitude about the weather reflects their feelings about other areas of life and encourages them to put off negative thought patterns and put on positive ones.

Like Jesus, the Danes seem to recognize that true contentedness is deeply connected to rootedness—to know who and whose you are. Social posturing, competition, and comparison are quite uncommon in their culture. Instead, they tend to lead their lives with reciprocity, harmony, and service. *Hygge* helps nurture that perspective, allowing them to see that satisfaction will never come from the stuff they accumulate in their spaces but from the lives that they live there. The Joneses don't exist in Denmark, so there's never any urgency to keep up with them or anyone else, for that matter. A "go big or go home" attitude cannot coexist with contentment. The Danish determination to place value on people instead of possessions brings balance to the social hysteria of stockpiling and holding out for "the next best thing."

Simple pleasures cultivate contentment.

The Danes seem to understand the importance of gratitude. Their slower lives allow them to evaluate and savor moments so they don't take people, experiences, or even material possessions for granted. They give extra consideration to what is already right in front of them, leaving less room in their lives for wanting something or someone else.

Hygge favors the ordinary and familiar. It is unpretentious and imperfect and encourages satisfaction in everydayness. This attitude of gratitude helps them ignore the urge to reach for more. Many Danes quickly admit that having too much of anything undermines its value. Extravagance begins to feel exhausting and overwhelming when it happens all the time. Simple pleasures, on the other hand, cultivate contentment.

A CHANGE OF PERSPECTIVE

Of all the *hyggelige* tenets, contentment often seems the most difficult for me. Come October each year, when I see the numbers on the thermometer begin to plummet, my emotions threaten to descend into the depths too. I contemplate the plausibility of human hibernation, mentally declaring 1 Kings 1:1 my new life verse, "Now King David was old and advanced in years. And although they covered him with clothes, he could not get warm." I brace myself for the cabin fever that will inevitably come when I'm trapped indoors with five high-spirited children all the livelong day for the next nine months.

When the temperature becomes unbearable for outdoor play, my dining room will be converted into a roller-skating rink and my living room will be temporarily transformed into a WWF ring. I compare my current situation with my previous life in sunny Arizona and wonder why I chose to make my way to this wilderness of white in the first place.

But of course, I *could* move back to Arizona. I could move to Hawaii. I could move to Timbuktu. It wouldn't really matter. Despite the location of the patch of grass I call my own, it will never feel green enough or warm enough or fill-in-the-blank enough this side of the second Garden of heaven. That longing for something better or best is a remnant of Eden—a chronic case of heartburn that's been plaguing humanity since that first forbidden bite. Because you see, the enemy knew even then that if he couldn't steal our faith, he could at least try to distort our perspective.

Like Eve, we often assume that the flashy, just out of reach fruit is better. We look to the careers, the lifestyles, the homes (in my case, the weather) of others and assure ourselves that if we could only have what they have, we would be more than satisfied. Then we'd be content. We spend precious time waiting around for a someday life, not realizing that today is the most important day because it's the only one God has given for this moment. Instead of learning to observe and appreciate the ordinary, we grow disquiet and begin to compare our everyday fruit to what looks to be bigger and better things dangling off the branches of someone else's tree.

We fall prey to the social media selection bias. Instead of rejoicing with our friend who's been given a promotion, our neighbor whose son just received a full-ride scholarship to an Ivy League school, or that one online influencer we follow whose husband just surprised her with an anniversary trip to Spain, we allow their earthly success to become our spiritual downfall. Our dark insecurities bring our idols into the light. Regardless of how God has parted the water for us, all we can see is the boat He's provided for someone else.

Envy conveniently leaves out half the story, only allowing us to see a narrowed perspective of everyone else's life. We can't pin all of our troubles with contentment on comparisons; it is a more complicated equation than that. But all of humanity longs to be more like *this*, and less like *that*, to have more of *this* and less of *that*.

When this kind of discontent creeps in, overspending often

results. We excuse or belittle our excessive purchases, shrewdly categorizing them as a need instead of a want, so as not to feel guilty for our second-class stewardship. In the end, though, we find ourselves tangled in excess, suffering under the weight of financial gluttony and repeated exposure to "affluenza." The problem isn't the purchased item. The problem is the heart reason for why we purchased the item in the first place. It has been said that we do things we detest, to buy things we don't need, with money we don't have, to impress people we don't like.[1] Our tendency to make tally marks and tier levels out of virtually everything contributes greatly to our overall joylessness and discontent.

> *You and I don't need to be constantly seeking our best life. Instead, we can recognize that we're already living a pretty good one right now.*

These practices of discontentment are called a comparison "trap" for a reason. When we compare ourselves to anyone but Christ, we never come out unscathed.[2] Comparison is a two-edged sword. If we see our lives as a failure, we're going to be driven by guilt and shame. Those feelings are certainly not from God. On the flip side, if we see our lives as a success, we tend to puff up with pride—and that's not a godly response either. Our only hope is to fix our eyes on Jesus, the Author, Finisher, and Perfecter of our faith (Heb. 12:2). As Elisabeth Elliot once wrote, "The secret is Christ in me, not me in a different set of circumstances."[3] You and I don't need to be constantly seeking our best life. Instead, we can recognize that we're already living a pretty good one right now.

Frankly, we're not the only unsatisfied customers. A 2017 Gallup poll of more than 2.5 million Americans showed the largest decline of overall feelings of well-being (or joy) in the last ten years.⁴ Our friends and neighbors are struggling to keep their eyes on their own papers too. The devil has tempted them with self-preservation, self-promotion, and self-sufficiency—the same low-hanging fruit he tried serving up to Jesus. As followers of Christ, you and I can lead our loved ones out of the wilderness by leading them right to Him.

In an attempt to help her family do just that, author Kristen Welch serves beans and rice once a week for supper. This basic meal, albeit somewhat lackluster by American standards, is a staple for millions of people around the world. A weekly liturgy like this one helps curb complaints in Kristen's household by framing the experience with proper perspective. It forces them to observe the ordinary goodness of their lives and recognize that nothing they own is really theirs, including their meals. It's all been given to them by God. They are only stewards. "Nothing makes us more grateful than perspective," she writes.⁵ "If we're going to compare ourselves to those who have more, we must also compare ourselves to those who have less."⁶ This was the very path of Jesus as He made His way out of the wilderness. This perspective is the heart of a *hyggelig* home.

I'm not suggesting we eat only beans and rice for the rest of our lives. But establishing practices of simplicity into our *everyday* might nurture hearts of contentment in us and in others. Here are three simple suggestions that have helped me set my eyes on the right fruit.

Walk in truth. Through the clip-clap of my chattering teeth every winter, I can be heard echoing the sentiments of my Scandinavian friends, "No bad weather, only bad clothing." For sure, this well-meaning platitude falls short when I'm tempted to complain about non-weather-related struggles—the one bathroom that must be shared by seven people, the seventeen-year-old car that smells of wet dog, the girls' weekend getaway I was not invited to. No amount of warm clothing will soothe the ache of those disappointments. But there is some truth hiding in that little Danish refrain. Just as it reminds me to put on better clothing when I'm tempted to whine about the weather, it compels me to *put on* the right things at other times too. When I am met with a child who's caught in a lie, when my dishwasher breaks mid-cycle, when an unforeseen change in my work schedule cancels all my original plans—what do I put on then? Just as I have no authority over the weather, I can't control any of these things. I can, however, control what I put on in the midst of them. I can control my reactions.

The truth is, what we run *toward* matters just as much as what we run away *from*. We'll go where we gaze. If you and I are going to turn from our ever-present temptation of *self*, then, like Jesus, we need to turn toward truth. We need to have Scripture ever ready, speaking it to ourselves and over our circumstances. Arming ourselves with anything else is like bringing a stick to a sword fight. According to Ephesians 6:16–17, God's Word is my best weapon against the enemy and his wily ways: "In all circumstances take up the shield of faith, with which you can extinguish all the flaming darts of the evil one; and take the helmet of salvation, and the sword of the Spirit, which is the word of God."

When I made the decision to move to a small town in Minnesota all those years ago, I had no idea what a wilderness it would turn out to be. I could never have guessed how lonely I would feel, how frozen my toes would get, and how hard my heart would turn when it felt like my pleas for change went unheard. *Why, God? Why must I live in this near-arctic Mayberry, of all places? Clearly, my skin is not thick enough for this place and my personality is not a good match for these people.* I didn't want to be here. I didn't belong.

I rationed my joy out in small little bites. I focused so much attention on what I thought was wrong with my life, never satisfied with where I was and what I'd been given, that I had little appetite left for anything but the disappointment. For the most part, I carried around a backpack full of decomposing fruit that weighed me down and left a bitter aftertaste.

As I learned more about *hygge*, however, it became easier and easier to do as the Danes do. I couldn't always choose my circumstances, but I could choose my perspective. I had a choice. Like the children of Israel, I could continue to wander in my wilderness of displeasure, stirring up a lot of dust but never really getting anywhere, or like Jesus, I could fight for contentment. *Why settle for death when life is possible?*

I chose the way of Jesus, searching the Scriptures for passages that would help me count the gains instead of grieving the losses. The ordinary everyday was my problem. I didn't wish to win the lottery. I wasn't secretly pining for a trip to Paris. I just wanted to get through today without always longing for tomorrow. I wanted to find joy in the here and now. For that reason, I had to be in the Word every day. I had to devour Scripture until I could taste and see that the Lord is good.

That didn't mean I packed up all my dreams. God wasn't asking me to. He's only ever asked that I tend the garden He's given me so I don't allow the fruit of

> *Scripture reminds me that I am God's workmanship. . . . When I find myself groping for better or best instead of the good God has given me, I return to His Word to put on a renewed perspective.*

discontent to ripen into entitlement. He wants me to faithfully steward all of my life—the stuff He's given me, the place and time He's ordained for me, the opportunities He's sent my way, but also my attitude about all of those things. Learning to be content about the weather is a huge part of my surrender since moving to Minnesota, but it's not my only struggle. Each day I have to fight the urge to complain about many things, like my home decor, my career, the academic success of my kids, my health, my hairstyle, my weight. Scripture reminds me that I am God's workmanship, created anew in Christ for the good works God prepared for me from the very beginning (Eph. 2:10). When I find myself groping for better or best instead of the good God has given me, I return to His Word to put on a renewed perspective.

So, should you pass me on the street some arctic day in April and hear me muttering under my breath, know that I'm silently rehearsing some truth like the Little Engine That Could. I'm re-calibrating my heart with Philippians 4:11: "For I have learned, in whatsoever state I am, therewith to be content" (KJV). *I can be content in the state of Minnesota. I can be content in the state of Minnesota. I can be content.* Put off. Put on.

Serve others. Last weekend when most of their peers were still nestled in bed sleeping off the sediment of a reckless Friday night, my oldest kids were on the other side of town, unloading crates of day-old produce and pantry staples. They stacked them on tables in the basement of an aging church. Joining a handful of other volunteers, they sorted out wilting lettuce and dented cans of baked beans, packaging the remaining items in to-go boxes for under-resourced families in our community.

This wasn't the first time my kids had found themselves elbow-deep in bulk jars of peanut butter and nearly expired eggs. They've been serving at food pantries and soup kitchens since they were still in diapers, standing on stools, placing a cookie or a scoop of rice on a waiting meal tray. Now in their teens, they wake at too-early-o'clock a couple of times a month and drive themselves over to that makeshift distribution center. The rest of the family joins them each fourth Saturday. We strap on stiff aprons and spend the morning cooking up industrial-sized pans of Sloppy Joes, spaghetti, tacos, or the like for anyone in need of a free hot lunch.

Don't allow my words here to give you the impression that my children are perfect. Often the call to serve others is eclipsed by their unceasing cries of discontent. But I can say the same of myself. We're all in progress, after all. But with the help of *hygge*, we are all learning that it is not what we gather in this lifetime that breeds contentment. It's what we give; it's how we serve. When we're busy sharing our talents, energies, and resources, we don't have time to think about ourselves and our circumstances.

Discontent gives way when we make room for openhanded stewardship. Gathering hygiene items for the homeless man who camps outside McDonald's every night makes us realize how fortunate we are to be among the 74 percent of people in the world who have daily access to running water.[7] Foregoing new gym shoes during back-to-school sales so we can purchase some for a classroom in Haiti discourages feelings of entitlement or greed. Organizing a monthly game night for the kids at a local woman's shelter so the moms can have a much-needed night out to themselves gives us a greater appreciation for the relatively easy

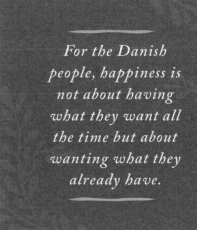

For the Danish people, happiness is not about having what they want all the time but about wanting what they already have.

lives we lead each day. Whenever we're tempted to feel like our load is too heavy, we volunteer to carry someone else's and we're quickly set straight. Serving provides perspective. Unity becomes the natural byproduct of being on mission together. When we have the same gospel goal, we end up reaching for Jesus at the same time. Our hands clasp His and inadvertently grab hold of each other's.

Live in gratitude. With the help of *hygge,* the Danes are generally optimistic people, taking a posture of gratitude, satisfaction, and positivity. That's not to say they never face hardships or less-than-ideal situations, but they've learned to be masters of spin. They've chosen to reframe their thoughts about their current circumstances to live more joyful lives. Gratefulness turns what they have into enough. For the Danish people, happiness is not about having what they want all the time but about wanting what they already have. It's about seeing their stuff through a new lens.

Hygge can help you name things differently too. For instance, the mound of dishes that greets you at the end of each evening—that's daily evidence that you have people in your life who eat at your table. The clean laundry pile that threatens to landslide all over your living room floor each time you pass is not an eyesore but a blessed reminder that you have clothes on your back. Your outdated living room couch is not so much a blemish on your decor as a memorial of the countless movie nights you've enjoyed with friends or Sunday afternoon naps you've savored.

I don't know what "bad weather" you are slogging through right now. Perhaps you are facing complicated family dynamics, an overbearing boss, some post-baby weight that you just can't seem to shed. No matter what is tempting you to feel justified in discontent, know this: feelings don't always tell the whole story. They can't always be trusted.

I have a lamppost at the edge of my front yard. It's a bit of an oddity in the neighborhood, hinting back to a different era, but it has always reminded me of the lamp that lights Lucy's way into Narnia. When I wake on a winter day to see it shining out over the white wonderland of snow, my breath catches. First snows, especially, can be beautiful and otherworldly. The first snows of winter *feel* like a gift—a playful dusting from the One who delights in giving us good things.

But come May, when there's *still* white covering my yard, I usually *feel* quite a bit different about the snow out there. In May, snow shouts to the world, "It's always winter and never Christmas." In May, a blessing feels more like a burden. The snow didn't change, mind you, but my feelings about it did.

Isn't that the way it is with the feelings of a fickle heart? Praise spills quickly from my lips when God's gift is convenient for me, when it is given according to my timetable, when it looks "good" through my eyes. But should His gift force me to rearrange my original plans, should it arrive later than I thought it ought, should it appear more painful than pleasurable, my praise comes out clipped or, sadly, not at all.[8]

Feelings of disappointment are not always inappropriate. The opposite of contentment is not the absence of desire, after all. But we must remember that feelings are really only a barometer that should lead us to find the truth about our circumstances. Our attitude about a situation reveals what we think we deserve.

Gratitude might seem too simple in an overcomplicated world. At the end of the day, you can only control two things: what you give to the world and your attitude about what the rest of the world has given you. Your friends and family need to see you living in gratitude. When you spend so much time grumbling about a current situation, you draw attention away from the presence and perfection of Jesus. You inadvertently proclaim that who He is and what He has provided is not enough.

The idea that God owes you or me anything beyond what He has already given us is a dangerous notion. From the beginning, He's given us abundantly more than we could ever ask for or imagine (Eph. 3:20). May our response to the good He's given echo the words of the prophet Habakkuk, "Though the fig tree should not blossom, nor fruit be on the vines, the produce of the olive fail and the fields yield no food, the flock be cut off from the fold and there be no herd in the stalls, yet I will rejoice in the LORD; I will take joy in the God of my salvation" (Hab. 3:17–18).

If you're having trouble voicing your gratefulness, remember that while practice doesn't always make perfect, it does make progress. Sometimes in life, you just have to play scales over and over until you get better, until the noise starts to sound like music. In this case, you have to keep saying "Thank you" until you actually mean it. Find one particular verse of thanksgiving in the Bible and pray it back to the Lord. Record one or two thoughts in a gratitude journal each day. Or better yet, write them all out on individual slips of paper and place them in a jar. Each time you're tempted to complain, reach for one of the slips and recount your praise instead.

NOT YET HOME

"Danes stay happy in winter because it's so awful outside that coming home inspires an overwhelming rush of relief and gratitude at having survived the elements," writes expat Helen Russell in *The Year of Living Danishly*.[9] As Christians, we've not come home yet. The inkling of unease we feel in our souls is sometimes a longing for something better. It's a hope of heaven calling to us. But we can't allow seeds of discontent to sprout and grow into self-centered dissatisfaction. We're promised eternal perfection,

CONTENTMENT

like Christ's, someday. For now, we need to find ways to be grateful for *what is* instead of always looking ahead to *what if*.

Our friends and neighbors will learn that "the earth is the LORD's and the fullness thereof, the world and those who dwell therein" (Ps. 24:1) when they see us finding satisfaction in the providence of God and good fruit He has set before us. In our daily, repetitive faithfulness—one breath at a time, one meal at a time, one prayer at a time—let us change our perspective. Let's walk in truth, serve others, and live with gratitude. Let's not waste another minute complaining about the weather. Let's just learn to put on better clothes.

—— CONSIDERING CONTENTMENT ——

1. Which part of the unholy trinity of self do you struggle to relinquish the most: self-preservation, self-promotion, or self-sufficiency?

2. What "better" fruit do you find yourself reaching for lately?

3. What "bad weather" currently plagues you? What verses can you "put on" to help shift your words from complaints to praise?

4. Who needs your time, talent, and energy today? How can you best serve them?

5. Look around at your everydayness. Name three mundane parts that might need reframing. How can you praise God for those things?

—— TASTE AND SEE ——

- Philippians 4:11
- Psalm 4:7–8
- 1 Timothy 6:6–10
- Matthew 6:25–34
- Romans 8:32

——— A PRAYER FOR CONTENTMENT ———

Heavenly Father, I realize my discontent reveals my ingratitude for who You are and what You have provided. I repent of my selfishness and ask You to renew a right spirit in me. Give me a proper perspective about my circumstances. When I'm tempted to complain, help me recall a verse of praise. Show me how I might use my time, talent, and resources to serve others. Thank You for always providing the fruit I need. Amen.

REST

Beware of the barrenness of a busy life!

BISHOP J. TAYLOR SMITH

For six whole days, God masterfully crafted a sanctuary that would reveal His glory. For six whole days, He worked. But by the seventh day, His work was finished. It wasn't just done. It was complete, lacking nothing. In response, He rested. With purpose, God set aside His work, and in turn, set apart the day. The seventh was unlike the previous six; it was holy. In the same way He had blessed the animals and humans, God blessed the day of rest. Animals, people, and the day of rest—all would be fruitful and would multiply the life-giving work He had started in that Garden home.

God's posture of rest was not without His continued provision, however. His was a pause of work, not a pause of care. While resting, He continued to uphold His creation, maintaining it, loving it, and communing with it. God was neither lazy nor tired. He was not worn out; He was wise. His rest would serve as both an example and a permission slip for centuries to come, reminding humanity of their fragility and their need for restoration.

Even before the official institution of a rest day, so much of creation already whispered this work-rest design. With every contraction and release of muscle, Adam's heart declared the goodness of work and rest. With every steady inhale and faithful exhale of his lungs, his breath proclaimed that pausing was necessary. From the rising and setting of the sun to the dependable turning of the seasons, all of creation revealed a work-rest rhythm.

Still, God knew Adam and Eve would require further proof of their need for rest. In His final display of creativity, the Creator paused His *doing* for an entire day and declared that He was done, affirming the idea that work had a purpose, but that rest did too.

THE REST OF JESUS

As an observant Jew, a rabbi no less, Jesus knew the Levitical laws concerning rest. The customs of Shabbat, or Holy Sabbath, had been passed down from His ancestral line for nearly forty generations. In Hebrew, *shabbat* means to "cease" or "desist from labor" and was first fully observed by the wandering children of Israel (Exodus 16).[1] In the wilderness, they were instructed to gather only a day's worth of manna each morning, an *omer* per person. By the first sunrise, fearing the supply would eventually dwindle or that perhaps God would forget to provide the next day's meal, the people disregarded His clear instructions and began to stockpile extra manna for the days to come. By daybreak the following morning, their reserves were covered with maggots and emitting a foul stench that spread throughout the camp. Having learned a valuable lesson in obedience, they conceded to the warning of Moses,

"Let no one leave any of it over till the morning" (Ex. 16:19).

This daily practice continued until the sixth day when God offered different directions—a new command to test the trust of the people. "Tomorrow is a day of solemn rest, a holy Sabbath to the Lord; bake what you will bake and boil what you will boil, and all that is left over lay aside to be kept till the morning" (Ex. 16:23). As God's spokesman, Moses ordered the people to gather two portions of manna on Friday. They were to eat one and save the other for the following day, the Sabbath. They'd not have to spend the last day of the week gathering and preparing food. In this way, God was granting them a day of rest—a day to cease. Even more, God was building their faith in His ability to provide. He was teaching them the concept of *enough*—the idea that He would give them exactly what they needed when they needed it. Ceasing their work would allow them to learn to trust Him both with their plenty and with their lack.

Sometime later, God's command to rest was written in stone, formally instituting specific practices of Shabbat: "Remember the Sabbath day, to keep it holy. Six days you shall labor, and do all your work, but the seventh day is a Sabbath to the Lord your God. On it you shall not do any work, you, or your son, or your daughter, your male servant, or your female servant, or your livestock, or the sojourner who is within your gates" (Ex. 20:8–10). It was not by accident that this particular mandate was number four in the line-up of God's laws. By its strategic placement, the Sabbath became a bridge between the first three commandments, which referred to the people's relationship with God, and the last six, which spoke of their relationships with each other. It was a tool to help them connect with both. The command, mercifully, put everyone, no matter their socioeconomic background, on an equal plane. Everyone was to rest—men and women, sons and daughters, servants, livestock, visitors. If the rich rested, spending their time communing with God instead of working, they allowed the poor among them to do the same. No one was excluded.

But God's restoration extended beyond just that one day. He went on to declare that in addition to the seventh-day Sabbath, the people were to celebrate an extended rest every seven years. The Year of Release, or *shmita,* became a rest for the land when the fields were left fallow so they could recover (Lev. 25:1–7). As always, the poor were then encouraged to glean any free-growing crops that remained, providing for those who lacked the means to help themselves (Lev. 19:9–10).

Every seven cycles of *shmita* ushered in the Year of Jubilee— an entire year of Sabbath-like restoration. Slaves were released. Debts were forgiven. Land was reinstated to original owners (Lev. 25:8–16). In this way, Sabbath economy not only supported environmental friendliness but also social justice. Rest wasn't just a chance to take a break, it was a way of stewarding creation and honoring the poor. It was God's gift to His people, a sign of freedom for those who had been born into slavery and had never had a day off. There at the base of Mt. Sinai, God's command was a reflection of that perfect Garden home, a sign throughout the generations that their dwelling place was the Lord (Ex. 31:13). Even though they were nomads, wandering the

> *For centuries, the religious elite had twisted God's Sabbath law so much that the liberty it was meant to provide a freed people felt more like the shackles of slavery they had left behind. Jesus came to shift the focus from a rule to a relationship.*

wilderness, Sabbath gave them a home in Him.

This was the rest that Jesus knew. This was the rest of His people. In accordance with the law and in the shadow of generations before Him, Jesus refrained from doing thirty-nine different types of work from sunset on Friday to sunset on Saturday.[2] This often comes as a surprise to many Christians. When they look at Scripture through modern eyes, some mistakenly see a rebellious Jesus who flouted the law and ignored the authority of the religious leaders. To them, He was a freedom fighter, a renegade. In some ways He was. But most of all He was an obedient Son—one who didn't come to abolish the law His Father had established but to fulfill it.

For centuries, the religious elite had twisted God's Sabbath law so much that the liberty it was meant to provide a freed people felt more like the shackles of slavery they had left behind. Jesus came to shift the focus from a rule to a relationship. His rest would fully restore.

HYGGE REST

Americans, especially, need the kind of rest only Christ can provide. We are speed addicts. We're all gas and no brakes. According to a recent study of US "knowledge workers," 87 percent of us log more than forty hours of work each week.[3] We toil right through our lunch breaks, slip into the office on weekends to catch up, and opt out of coveted paid time off. On average, we work four and a half weeks longer each year than the generation before us.[4] Even when we are at home, we are never truly off the clock.

Since 2007 when the first iPhone and the global expansion of Facebook and Twitter ushered in the digital age, we've had constant access to our office in our back pocket. Work goes with us wherever we go. We check email before our feet hit the floor in the morning and scroll through the latest tweets at the breakfast table. We check the status of a work order while using the bathroom. We answer phone calls via Bluetooth during our morning commute. We're in the office mentally long before we ever get there physically. The end of the day doesn't fare much better. We bring our work, and really the whole world, home with us every evening. Our phones never pause. Consequently, neither do we. We rebel against rest because it feels like laziness or wasted potential. We assume that more time spent working will mean increased productivity. Unfortunately, we've been misinformed.

After extensive research for the Stanford Institute for Economic Policy Research, Professor John Pencavel concluded that productivity greatly decreases after a fifty-hour work week. Fatigue and stress intensify, increasing on-the-job errors, accidents, and illness and ultimately negating any gains that may have been made.[5]

In stark contrast to Americans who fast-walk through life, the Danish people don't mind taking things slow. To them, rest is not a four-letter word. Then again, neither is work. The Danes strike a healthy balance between the two. Their official work week is only thirty-seven hours long with some reports coming in as low as thirty-four. With thirteen days off for public holidays and five weeks of paid leave, the Danes average eighteen and a half days of work per month.[6] These shorter bursts of productivity mean that businesses close earlier. Commercial districts go dark. Parking lots sit empty. Instead of toiling from nine to five, the Danes head home around three in the afternoon.

This intentional dormancy and healthy work-life balance is especially common in the winter months. From November to February, *hygge* envelopes the Danish people, wrapping them both physically and metaphorically in a seasonal cocoon. The Danes turn inward, slow down, and focus their energies on their home and communities. Outsiders are quick to criticize this social hibernation, calling it exclusive and insular. This desire to gather close with those you love and provide a safe and restful space indoors is often misconstrued as unwelcoming and stolid. Entire towns sit idle. Whole neighborhoods begin to winter. But *hygge* isn't a shutting out. It's a gathering in. Critics have also called this slower, more leisurely lifestyle *bourgeois* and *privileged*. But the Danes don't see it that way. To them, *hygge* is not a careless use of time. It's not accidental or reckless. It's a secular Sabbath in a world craving rest.

RELEASE AND RECEIVE

Like the Shabbat celebrated by Christ, *hyggelig* rest is intentional and is designed to encourage you to stop holding your breath. It's an exhale, a release without which you'd have no room left in your life to receive. This simple posture of rest is deliberate surrender. It's a discipline and an act of humility.

As women, we live hurried lives. Our days are long, and our to-do lists are even longer. We often feel tossed into the deep end, and we never seem to have enough time or energy to come up for air. Our physical and mental busyness has spiritual repercussions. We're asphyxiating our souls.

That last statement may come across rather heavy-handed, especially for approval junkies, like me. For the overachievers,

> We scratch and claw our way to the approval of others, convinced that without our arms holding the whole thing up, the world would crumble. This should compel us to ask: Whose "Well done" are we working for?

the efficiency addicts, the serial finishers, rest can feel like an anchor. *How dare we hit pause when there is still so much to be done?* But if we could slow down long enough and finally stop tapping our foot, we'd see our busyness isn't the real issue. It's only a symptom of a deeper problem: pride.

Hurry has become a tool of the enemy, convincing us to wear our work like a badge of honor. Work makes us feel significant, needed, irreplaceable. *If I don't do this task, who will? Who can?* we privately wonder. We deceive ourselves into believing that since we're busy, we must be more important than we actually are. We must have a purpose. As if the two labels are synonymous. We scratch and claw our way to the approval of others, convinced that without our arms holding the whole thing up, the world would crumble. This should compel us to ask: Whose "Well done" are we working for?

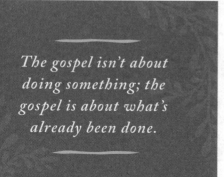

The gospel isn't about doing something; the gospel is about what's already been done.

Christian women are especially susceptible to the soul-jaundicing effects of hustle. We work under the reckless notion that our cheeks need to be flushed in heaven from the labor we've done here on earth. We are rest-avoidant because, at some point, some well-meaning someone had us all believing that the central aim of our lives is to be useful to God, but it's not. We're meant to glorify God. *That's* our purpose. The end.

Yes, there's work to be done, but most of the results have very little to do with our effort. We may plant the seed, but we can't control how quickly it breaks into a bud. We can't govern the timing of the rain. At some point, we have to lay down our tools and just wait for the hidden work of God. We have to rest and rely on Him, trusting that He'll grow a great harvest out of our few tiny seeds.

Isn't that freeing? Especially to those of us who want to use our lives, our homes, our *hygge* to point others to Jesus? We might feel like the outcome of our kingdom work is up to us—but it's not. The gospel isn't about doing something; the gospel is about what's already been done. In our commitment to creating a place for the gospel to grow, we can't forget that the rest Christ provides is not just for us to share with others; it's for us to enjoy as well.

Author Edith Schaeffer wrote that a home should have a door with both a hinge and a lock.[7] In other words, just as the Danish people intentionally close up during the quiet months of winter, knowing that dormancy is necessary, we need to protect our homes from overuse. We can't have an open door all the time. Learning when to close it to the outside world to provide restoration for those inside is just as important for kingdom work as learning when and how to open the door. We can feel free to use the lock. We can rest because of the completed work of Jesus. In that way, Sabbath is a test of our trust in Him, not just with our ministry but with our very lives.

Just as the wandering Israelites had to trust God to keep the double portion of manna fresh on the Sabbath, you must have

> *When you intentionally set aside a portion of your week to ignore the urgent emails, let the dishes pile up in the sink, and disregard that time-consuming errand, you're not being lazy. You're confidently placing the tasks of tomorrow into God's hands and confessing that His grace is sufficient for today.*

faith in God's ability to sustain you by obediently forfeiting your labor for a time. When you intentionally set aside a portion of your week to ignore the urgent emails, let the dishes pile up in the sink, and disregard that time-consuming errand, you're not being lazy. You're confidently placing the tasks of tomorrow into God's hands and confessing that His grace is sufficient for today.

Who you turn to when the stakes are high—when the responsibilities are mounting—says a lot about whom you trust. Sabbath rest is a tithe of time allowing you to release the burden of a completed to-do list to God and receive the gift of His favor for your obedience (Isa. 58:13–14). That's not to say that when you rest your tasks will magically disappear. Like the boy who brought his small offering of five loaves and two fish on a hillside so many years ago, when you rest in obedience, you'll watch as Christ takes your time rations and multiplies them. Nothing will ever be done in half measures on His watch. Water will be turned into wine. Oil will be poured from empty jars. Empty nets will be filled to overflowing. He'll make a way when there is no way.

Admittedly, there are seasons of life when rest is elusive. Sabbath can feel like a chore to a mother of young kids, especially one who's convinced that the world will collapse if she stops turning it. No matter how well she orchestrates the other six days of the week, she knows diapers will still need to be changed, spills will

> *Like the boy who brought his small offering of five loaves and two fish on a hillside so many years ago, when you rest in obedience, you'll watch as Christ takes your time rations and multiplies them.*

still require a mop, sick children will still command her attention on her day of rest. The unavoidable responsibilities of motherhood can cause her to grow increasingly irritable, resentful, and anxious. Can you relate? If so, be mindful not to confuse *care* with *work*. They are not the same things. Perhaps that's why God continued to hold up creation on that seventh day of rest. Nothing faded or fell away under His watchful eye.

Likewise, Jesus never let the law get in the way of His love for the people. By His command, blind eyes were opened and lame legs began to walk, even on Shabbat. As Lord of the Sabbath, Christ chose *that* day to cast out evil spirits, heal the sick, and forgive sins. His ministry was not contrary to the rest God required. Nothing could have been more restorative than the care He provided. His example should remind us that those placed under our charge will still need our care even while we rest. Be careful not to allow your desire to rest warp into a demand for it. Release your congested schedule to Him and wait with your arms outstretched. Release. Receive.

THE WORK OF REST

For years, I understood *why* I needed to release my schedule and rest but had no working knowledge of *how* to do it. Like Eve, I pridefully assumed I could take on the world, do it all, be as God. Granted, I would never have said those words out loud. But my actions said what my lips wouldn't voice. I was an efficiency addict, chasing the high of a completed checklist. My busyness started out as a brush fire but eventually grew into a raging inferno. Somewhere between homeschooling my four kids, leading a Bible study at church, co-coordinating a homeschool co-op, managing an online business, and writing for a local women's magazine, I found out

I was pregnant with my fifth child. Publicly I rejoiced over the gift of this new life, but privately, I grieved over the second-class mothering I was convinced this baby would endure. I was emotionally and physically bankrupt. I didn't have enough wiggle room in my schedule for the full-time responsibility another child would surely be. My life was rearranging itself by the day, and I didn't know how to untangle the mess. I needed rest, and I needed it yesterday.

How could I continue to be a good wife, mother, friend, and neighbor when I was so tired? How could I share the love of Christ with others when my soul felt malnourished? What I didn't realize is that the idea of "You are what you eat" applies to both physical and spiritual appetites. In my refusal to rest—to lay aside my work in order to worship the Lord—I was starving my soul.

Up until that point, *hygge* had buoyed me well enough. The calming aesthetics, comforting relationships, and overall slowness of a *hyggelig* lifestyle provided a certain level of peace and contentment to my home. Yet I still ended so many days feeling depleted. No amount of ambient lighting or chamomile tea seemed to satisfy my need for sanctuary. All my worst moments—when I was parched, brittle, and looked the least like Christ to others—happened when I was too busy, when I had packed my schedule so tightly that I spent my week rushing instead of truly resting. I knew that *hygge* could only ever be a counterfeit of the Sabbath I desperately needed, but I was stuck. I had never been taught how to rest well.

> *Resting in Christ is not a distraction from the big work of the kingdom. It is the work of the kingdom.*

Perhaps, like me, you didn't get your faith handed to you. If

REST

that's the case, then you probably have secretly viewed Sabbath rest as waste, a bore, or even an indulgence you can't afford. But the truth is, resting in Christ is not a distraction from the big work of the kingdom. It *is* the work of the kingdom. Among all the spiritual disciplines mentioned in the Scripture, rest is the only one consecrated holy. It's time set aside "to the Lord" (Ex. 16:23). It's a time of worship. So why does time off sometimes feel like a punishment? If Sabbath was made for man, as Christ said in Mark 2:27, why doesn't it feel like the *good* that God declared it to be in Genesis chapter 2? Maybe it's because you're resting all wrong.

To be clear, Sabbath should not be practiced from a place of legalism. The moment we start asking, "What can or can't I do while I rest?" we miss the point altogether. Admittedly, rules give us a false sense of security. The idea that God is pleased by our performance and that He'll have a bigger blessing for the one who can check off the most boxes on a Sabbath list is, of course, what compelled the Pharisees to add more to God's simple instruction in the first place. Rules aren't necessary, but sometimes it is helpful to know what rest actually looks like in order to know how best to embrace it.

To begin, remember that rest is not a suggestion. It is a command. As with financial offerings, Sabbath rest should be given from the first fruits—the best—of your time. Sabbath is intentional. It's not time that is taken from you. You're to relinquish it freely. I appreciate author Keri Wyatt Kent's explanation of planned rest: "Pausing is not the same as collapsing. Some people say, 'I'll do all my pausing at the end of the day, after the kids are in bed.' That's not hitting the brakes; that's running out of gas. Both get you stopped, but only one is intentional. And only one will help you feel more rested and peaceful."[8]

Perhaps that's why the Hebrew day begins at sunset. God knew all the way back in the Garden how important it was for the rest to come first: "And there was evening and there was morning, the first day" (Gen. 1:5). By Jewish standards, for the first half of the day, our lives are spent in the dark dormancy of night. We're resting. Make no mistake, however, resting is not just inactivity. Much is happening during that intentional pause. It's actually at night that our bodies heal, grow, and mend. Our brains sort and process the day, hormones flood our cells, our immune system releases infection-fighting proteins, and our muscles get a chance to relax and restore.[9] God does some of His best work while we rest.

It's no surprise, then, that the root of *shabbat* is a verb.[10] It's an action. Resting well takes work, not just from God, but from us too. Like the Israelites who cleaned their homes, gathered a double portion of manna, and made ready their hearts for worship in preparation for their Sabbath rest, you and I have to plan for it too. We can't allow it to just happen. Rest is not an accident. Sabbath isn't just another day off. Therefore, it demands our attention and—dare I say it?—our work. Hebrews 4:10–11 puts it this way: "Let us therefore strive to enter that rest, so that no one may fall by the same sort of disobedience." We are to strive toward rest. Other translations use words like "make every effort," "endeavor," and "labor." Your rest should have a purpose. It should draw you to love God and love others well. Unfortunately, when you've been running ragged for so long, it becomes harder and harder to remember how to walk with God.

If you've been going in the fast lane for too long, you have to slow down slowly. You have to apply the brakes properly. Otherwise, you'll just end up with whiplash. The truth is, coming to a hard stop is like putting a Band-Aid over a bullet hole. That kind of rest is a quick-fix Sunday solution that will only leave you feeling further and further behind come Monday morning. When your projects get pushed back, creating tighter deadlines and longer workdays, you'll begin to grow resentful and avoid resting altogether. When you plan for Sabbath with intention, however, you can hold your schedule out as an offering, not be forced to release it at scriptural gunpoint.

Start by freeing up parts of the other six days in order that your Monday *yes* doesn't equal a Sunday *yes* when commitments unexpectedly have to be pushed onto your day of *no*. You have to be willing to live six days differently in order to fully enjoy the seventh. That's not to say that your rest has to happen on Sunday to "count." For some, especially those who work in full-time vocational ministry, resting on Sunday isn't an option. But if you can't rest on Sunday, you should rest on some day each week.

Before agreeing to join this committee or volunteering to complete that task, determine how those responsibilities will affect your Sabbath rest. Additionally, it's helpful to follow the time sequence set by God. Start your Sabbath the night before, perhaps right after dinner. Set aside your work until the following dinner hour, creating a night-day pattern for your rest. In that way, you will still leave enough time at the end of your Sabbath to organize the week and prepare for the busy day ahead.

> *Sabbath rest should look different from everyday slowness. True rest implies worship and restoration, savoring the presence of the Lord.*

By waging a one-woman war on your workweek, refusing to take on too many additional responsibilities, you are actually going to battle against the enemy. You are laying down your right to do more than you want in order to have the time to do what you ought. Unlike Eve when she took that bite of forbidden fruit, you are acknowledging that you are a limited being, waiving your desire to be like God. Rest, then, is less about self-care and more about self-denial.[11]

No matter how busy or free you feel in your current season, Sabbath rest should look different from everyday slowness. True rest implies worship and restoration, savoring the presence of the Lord. But rest is not limited to prayer and praise. It involves relaxation too. Rest is not the passive leisure of entertainment. Instead, restful activities should fill in all the desolate places of your mind, body, and emotions. They should refuel and repair your soul.

Rest will obviously look different for everyone and in every season. The activities that your friend finds restful and what helps set her heart toward worship and praise to God might be totally different from what gives your soul rest. Likewise, what you found restorative in your single years might be completely draining after you've gotten married or have had children. For instance, I currently like to play worship music, cozy up with a good book, or do some just-for-fun baking to recharge. In this season, these simple *hyggelige* practices feel like a deep breath to my asthmatic days. But all of those activities would have been about as helpful to me as bloodletting back when I had three babies in diapers. In those days, what I needed most was a nap. Similarly, I have a friend who likes to garden while she observes the Sabbath. But rooting around in the dirt would feel like a forced community service sentence to me. It is never well with my soul after I've done any amount of gardening. Fortunately, in His kindness, God allows us both to choose how best to rest. All He asks is that we make the day different and set apart from all the others, offering up our time as a sweet fragrance of obedience to Him.

THE YOKE OF REST

If your current situation has you feeling overwhelmed and under-staffed, unsure how to find rest in your symphony of chaos, re-member that God sees your weak and worn-out places. He knows you're fragile. He's heard your threadbare prayers. You may not know where to place your hand to stop the bleeding, but He does. His answer to your bruised and battered soul is found in Matthew 11:28–30: "Come to me, all who labor and are heavy laden, and I will give you rest. Take my yoke upon you, and learn from me, for I am gentle and lowly in heart, and you will find rest for your souls. For my yoke is easy, and my burden is light." These were the words of Jesus, spoken to a crowd of people whose daily cries for restoration tore from their throats in anguished whispers. His rest was for the weary ones.

In the agrarian society of ancient Israel, the term *yoke* had three meanings, all of which applied to the kind of help and hope the people needed and that we still need today.

Yoke: wooden bar or frame used to join draft animals at the heads or necks so that they pull together.[12] When they heard the word *yoke*, the Israelites were often inclined to think of its most straightfor-ward meaning.

The Jewish farmer would tether two oxen in order that their labor could be combined. Two animals were essentially tasked to do the same job. Their united effort would get the job done a lot faster and more efficiently. The yoked oxen didn't always carry the responsibilities equally, however. Occasionally, when a farmer needed to break in a new ox, he'd yoke it to a seasoned one. The more mature animal would carry the most weight and would lead his untrained companion in the way he should go. The older ox supplied the force. The newer one just had to follow.[13] When imploring the people to take His yoke upon them, Jesus was providing Himself as the seasoned ox. He was volunteering to carry the burden of their day, their week, their lifetime. Mercifully, He's offering us the same yoke. The enemy wants us to believe we can and should be able to hold up all things—our marriages, our kids, our friendships, our houses, our work, our ministries, and even our relationship with God, but we can't. We'll never be strong enough to carry all of that. When we rest, however, we place those responsibilities on Christ. We no longer have to strain under the weight of them. He's strong enough to carry them all.

But a wooden harness was just one of the pictures Jesus was painting in the minds of the Israelites that day. There were two more meanings of the word *yoke* that begged their attention.

Yoke: adopting Torah.[14] To the Jewish people, a yoke was a rabbinic interpretation and application of the Old Testament law. Wearing a yoke was a disciple's willing submission and agreement with a rabbi's particular teachings.[15] The fact that Jesus had a yoke is not unusual. Every rabbi had one. Every rabbi still does. What makes Christ's different is the fact that it was easy. His teaching on how to live life, love God, dwell in community, spend money, manage time, labor at work was easy. It wasn't without trouble, mind you, but it was easy. It still is. When followed, His yoke will lead to rest. When your time is not dictated by pride, greed, mismanagement of resources, or laziness,

> When your time is not dictated by pride, greed, mismanagement of resources, or laziness, but instead is mandated by the Christlike qualities of humility, generosity, stewardship, and service, you can rest without regret.

but instead is mandated by the Christlike qualities of humility, generosity, stewardship, and service, you can rest without regret.

Christ's promise of an easy yoke echoes the words of the prophet Isaiah when he wrote, "But they who wait for the LORD shall renew their strength; they shall mount up with wings like eagles; they shall run and not be weary; they shall walk and not faint" (Isa. 40:31). *Wait* here means "to bind together."[16] Are you starting to see a pattern? When we wait on the Lord—when we yoke or bind ourselves to Him, we're no longer defined by weariness. We find rest.

The final depiction of the word *yoke* was perhaps the most provocative to the listeners that day—one that harkened back to the book of Exodus and the original command God had given to them.

Yoke: any burden of bondage as that of slavery.[17] The Jews had been yoked in Egypt for years. Only when God led them out of captivity did they get to savor the sweet gift of rest. And the rest was not just for certain Jews; it was for all Jews. Rest was for everyone—both the haves and the have nots. To the impoverished, the silence of rest was a powerful statement. In contrast to the selfish Garden choice of Eve whose consumption was a way of building her own kingdom, the intentional preparation of the Israelites all throughout the week made it possible for them to consume less on the Sabbath. For one whole day, shops were closed. Commerce came to a halt. Just as it is in Denmark today, those at the top of the economic food chain relinquished their rights to have it all and have it now. For one whole day, *hygge* was available to everyone. Sabbath was God's way of honoring those who didn't have enough, those who were still enslaved to poverty. It was His way of leveling the playing field and bringing a small bit of Garden-like justice to the world.

Years later, when they heard Jesus reference an easy yoke, no doubt, many of the Jews recalled the cruelty of the Egyptians who had enslaved their ancestors for generations. Their yoke had been hard. Their burden had been heavy. Although they had been granted their freedom during those wandering years, they were still enslaved. Their sin held them captive.

The truth is, sin still keeps people in bondage today—maybe your family, your friends, your neighbors. They need to know Jesus fulfilled the law and became their emancipation proclamation. When we pause our lustful consumption for a time, prioritizing our errands on a different day of the week, we allow and even encourage producers to rest also. We resist our urge to treat the oppressed as a commodity. We help release those ensnared by the modern-day slave trade and give them the honor they deserve. When we understand that sometimes the best way to minister to the world is to shut our doors and allow Christ to minister to us through His Word and our delight in Him, our restoration pours out to everyone around us. But most importantly, when we trade the bondage of busyness for His easy yoke, we display our deliverance and the One who granted it. We give them a glimpse of the eternal *hygge* that is theirs for the taking. In that way, Sabbath becomes freedom day for us and for them.

CONSIDERING REST

1. Out of the following list, which often contributes to your inability to rest: pride, greed, mismanagement of time, or laziness?

2. Examine your weekly responsibilities. Which *yes* has contributed to your *no* to rest? What do you need to release to Jesus in order to receive His rest?

3. Who needs your restorative care even on your day of rest? In what ways can your care of them reveal the hope of heaven?

4. Which definition of *yoke* was the most convicting to you? Why?

5. Make a list of three changes you might make in your current patterns of resting based on the example of Sabbath rest set in Exodus 16 and 20.

TASTE AND SEE

- Exodus 20:8–11
- Deuteronomy 5:12–14
- Psalm 127:1–2
- Isaiah 58:13–14
- Matthew 11:28–30
- Colossians 2:16–17
- Hebrews 4:1–11

A PRAYER FOR REST

Jesus, Your yoke is easy and Your burden is light. I feel overwhelmed by all the responsibilities groping for my attention. Help me not be ruled by pride. I confess I am insufficient and need Your help. Take my time. I surrender it to You, trusting You will accomplish whatever I am unable to bring about on my own. Show me what I need to release, and help me receive the rest that can only be found in You. May my habit of rest reveal a glimpse of Your eternal restoration to the world. Amen.

A HOME FOR
THE HOMELESS

We are all strangers in a strange land, longing for home.

MADELEINE L'ENGLE

rom the beginning, *home* has revealed the fingerprint of
God. Scattering the stars, He set the laws of the heavens.
Cupping the waters in His hand, He fixed the limits of the
waves. Measuring the foundation of the earth, He molded its foot-
ings and laid its cornerstone. From chaos and darkness came order
and light. And in the middle of it all, He made a garden, a home.
Here He welcomed His first guests with the open arms of hospitality. Here He built a relationship with them. Here He provided
comfort, contentment, and rest. The atmosphere of the Garden
was pretty, yes. But more importantly, it had an eternal purpose.

Home was made not for home's sake, but for the people who lived there. This is where they would be seen and known and loved.

Then sin entered the world and marred the perfection of that Garden home. Adam and Eve traded the blessing of home for the burden of homelessness. They were no longer welcome. Then again, neither was anyone else—not you, not me, not our neighbors nor our friends. Since that awful day when those first guests traded paradise for perdition, we've all been nomads, wandering in a desert of isolation, anxiety, and grief. Though the Garden was meant to swaddle everyone in sanctuary, sin left us wrapped in death.

But that wasn't the end of the story. Because of Christ, life became available once again. If you are in Him, then you're no longer a drifter doomed to die. You have a new Promised Land. And while that's great news, there's more. The truth is, Jesus didn't come to just give you an eternal home. He also came to show you how to live in the home you've got right now—to swing your doors wide open to make a home for the homeless, to build relationships that would draw others to Him. Your address here is only temporary, of course—just wood, hay, and stubble. It will one day pass away. But, in the meantime, the home you make in it can be one that will last forever.

MY HYGGE HOME

I was one of those nomads. When I left my migrant life in Phoenix to follow love all the way to the woods of central Minnesota, I had a house, but somehow it didn't feel like home. I was a stranger, desperately in need of shelter—not just for me but for my family and friends. In those lean years of marriage, when my bank account was so empty it practically had an echo, I went looking everywhere for Garden-like sanctuary.

In my search, I stumbled upon *hygge*, the cultural liturgy of my husband's family. Like their relations across the pond who have always faced relatively desolate and dreary conditions for much for the year, the Danish people of the Midwest have learned to find joy. Admittedly, they can't control all their circumstances, but with the help of a few *hyggelige* practices, they can almost always control their perspective. Like an archer who only has to move his arrow a fraction of an inch to change the entire trajectory of his shot, they know a few small alterations in their outer lives can make a surprising difference in their inner lives.

In those early days, *hygge* seemed like everything I never knew I always needed. Just hearing the word and all that it promised made my shoulders lift in excitement and then fall in exhale. I flew into a frenzy, snatching up all the *hygge* I could. Mine was a relentless pursuit of perfection. I bought the fuzzy socks and the flannel sheets. I baked the bread and dried the flowers. I threw the parties. I planned the outings. I lit the candles. I sat by the fire. At one point, I even took up knitting. (Somewhere there's a half-finished ball of knots trying desperately to look like a scarf. It's probably under the couch cushions, along with my dignity.) My efforts to make a cozy home grew to a fever pitch. Sadly, I can tell you it didn't stick, none of it.

Turns out, in my attempts at making *home*, I wasn't giving it the right name. My Promised Land was never meant to be found in a place. It was always to be found in a Person. Without the transforming work of Jesus, a cultural lifestyle would only ever be a placebo. When *hygge* offered candles, Christ offered light to the world. *Hygge* wrapped my weary self in wool. Christ wrapped me in significance and love. *Hygge* pulled out a leather chair so I could sit and just be. Christ stretched out His nail-scarred hands so I could belong. Truth be told, I longed for both. I knew *hygge* could help me make a pretty house. While *pretty* is never bad, when paired with life in Christ, it could be good. The combination of the two would help me turn a cozy house into a life-giving home.

After wasting many years complaining about my circumstances, I decided to mimic the Danes and change my perspective. It was then I realized God didn't get the address wrong when He moved me here to the Midwest. This is the home where I learned I'm not truly at home. Minnesota is my in-between—my momentary life between one perfect Garden and the next.

> *More often than not my entryway feels more like a mess than a mission field. But perhaps that's the whole point. It's the unremarkable and tarnished places that reveal and display the glory of Christ best.*

While I wait for that someday place, I'm here in this one, faithfully prioritizing the people who call this house their own and opening the doors wide to invite more in.

Granted, more often than not my entryway feels more like a mess than a mission field. But perhaps that's the whole point. It's the unremarkable and tarnished places that reveal and display the glory of Christ best. After all, when the angels announced the arrival of baby Jesus, they sent a ragtag band of social outcasts to a stable. The shepherds were drawn to that foul-smelling stall, Christ's first earthly home, because of how the angels talked about Him. The place was not impressive; Jesus was. Their message was "Good news! Great joy!" Be honest, when people talk about your home, what do they say? Is the testimony of your four walls one that is good news and great joy? Regardless of its imperfections, would your home reflect the One who can draw the shepherds of this world?

JUST OPEN THE DOOR

Opening the door is a sacred but ordinary act that can produce eternal dividends. Home is where people get to see a family for who they really are. When people walk into my home, they learn what it means to be an Erickson. They find the avalanching pile of shoes stacked by the door and a colorful rainbow of baseball caps hanging along the wall, revealing our divided loyalties on game days. They hear us call dibs on the coveted, oversized chair by the window every morning. They listen as our discussion turns into a debate and eventually into an argument. But they also witness us relinquish the chair to someone else without being asked or hear us say restorative words like "I'm sorry" and "I forgive you" when the conversation takes an ugly turn. They get to eat tacos smothered in French dressing, popcorn topped with maple syrup, or grilled peanut butter and jelly sandwiches—just a few of the accidental recipes we've grown to enjoy. They get to see our family culture, our Erickson-ness. Above all, it's here at our home that they witness a picture of the gospel. Home shows our deep, raw need and our ugliness, but it also displays the love of Christ lived out not in spite of our brokenness, but because of it.

Every time we invite others into our house, we have an opportunity to make them feel right at home. We help heal those whose home lives are anything but homey and make room for those who don't know where they belong.

Perhaps you remember the widower I mentioned, who made his way to our table one Thanksgiving night. He was a neighbor of a church friend and had no one with whom to spend the day. We started the meal as acquaintances, but by the time we scraped the last nibble of apple pie from our dessert plates, we felt like friends. Seven years later, just weeks before he donned a black suit to say "I do" to a sweet widow, he pulled my husband aside and said, "I just want you to know I'll never forget the love you and your family showed me during one of the toughest times of my life. I came to your table lonely. You provided a place among people. You gave me food, but more than that, you gave me hope for the future." All it took was one simple invitation, nothing flashy, nothing fancy, just an open door.

While cohosting a neighborhood block party potluck, I learned that a boy down the street was having trouble making friends at school. The fallout for his loneliness was aggressive outbursts, usually directed at his single mom, who had little to no support. The mother shared her concerns with me, a total stranger she had met only fifteen minutes before. With our paper plates piled high with four different kinds of macaroni salad and dips of all kinds, we introduced our sons to each other. Four years and one unexpected move later, the boys, now teens, are still great friends who've found ways to stay connected while living hundreds of miles apart. Our address may have changed, but our desire to guide this young man to the God who never changes has not.

Then there was the time our cramped living room was the backdrop for a woman from our church to feel safe enough to admit a past marital wound that hadn't healed properly. My husband and I were able to offer scriptural encouragement, prayer, and some friendly accountability.

However, we don't always say or do the right things when sharing Jesus with others. Not every conversation around here ends with a Bible verse. Like you, we're imperfect people, living in an imperfect world. But we've come to see our home as the perfect place where people can come to know God more just by entering. *Hygge* has given us the courage and know-how to say to the stranger, the lonely one, the friend or family member, "I see you. I know you. I love you. What's more, Jesus does too."

Though we did invite some of these weary ones to church, we didn't invite them all. They weren't all ready for the sometimes bewildering subculture of American church life. So instead, we invited them to our home. In doing so, we gave them a glimpse of the home they could have someday. After all, when Jesus could have used any analogy to describe His eternal kingdom, He didn't choose a giant arena with jumbotrons or a worship complex with all the shine of a Vegas casino. He didn't even choose a modest country chapel. He chose a *home:* "In my Father's house are many rooms. If it were not so, would I have told you that I go to prepare a place for you? And if I go and prepare a place for you, I will come again and will take you to myself, that where I am you may be also" (John 14:2–3). It's as if He was saying, "If you need me, look for me at home. It's where I'll be waiting for you."

Obviously, Jesus was referring to the home He's preparing in heaven. But, if you let them, His words can also be a commission for life on earth. It's here, at your home, you can offer your friends and family His Garden-like comfort and consolation. Here

> *It's not as if the gospel will not spread if we don't open our doors, but we'll be missing out on the opportunity to be a part of what God is doing if we don't. God welcomes us into His work. He invites us to invite others.*

is where you can welcome their hard things with your undivided attention. Your open door won't necessarily change their circumstances, but it can be the entry point for Jesus, who can change their perspective and eventually their lives.

In Charles Dickens's *A Christmas Carol*, the Ghost of Christmas Present invites a very broken Ebenezer Scrooge to a Christmas feast. His invitation was simple: "Come in! and know me better, man!"[1] Good conversation and connection awaited just across the threshold. The *hygge* lived out in a Christian's home goes one step further. It says, "Come in and know God better!" Granted, it's not as if the gospel will not spread if we don't open our doors, but we'll be missing out on the opportunity to be a part of what God is doing if we don't. God welcomes us into His work. He invites us to invite others.

> *Our friends and neighbors long for sanctuary. They reach for* hygge *because it promises the comfort and cozy that they crave, but what they really need is Christ.*

AT HOME WITH *HYGGE*

When Jesus left His home in heaven to make His home with us, it was a rescue mission. Jesus saw all the wandering ones, including you and me, and gave us a dwelling place: Himself. Now we can offer that same home to others. Our friends and neighbors long for sanctuary. They reach for *hygge* because it promises the comfort and cozy that they crave, but what they really need is Christ. May we open our arms in hospitality to draw them close in relationship with us and eventually with Him. May we care for them in the same way He's cared for us. May we model contentment no matter how harsh the winters might be, laying down our rights, our plans, and ourselves each and every day.

A home is important, it's true, but only because of the people gathered in it. It's not just where we live; it's who we love. Every person who enters your door has a divine appointment. When all the earth totters, your friends and neighbors can look to the unshakable refuge of your home to find hope. Here is where they can unleash their burdens and find real and lasting rest, where they can get a glimpse of the Garden God made. Here is where they can walk in and meet Jesus. Brick by brick, the house you build can show others how to find a home in Him. Obviously, *hygge* isn't necessary—but it certainly helps.

HYGGELIGE
ACTIVITIES FOR
GATHERING PEOPLE
AND GROWING
THE GOSPEL

There are many wonderful, practical ways to pair the outward help of *hygge* with the inward hope of Jesus. While some of these activities are seasonally specific, most can be enjoyed all year long. A few will help you nurture one of the seven tenets of *hygge* in the lives of your spouse, children, and roommates, but the rest will help you introduce *hygge* to your friends, neighbors, and strangers so you might one day introduce them to Christ.

EVERYDAY *HYGGE*

Curate a traveling blanket. Make or purchase a blanket. Each time your family takes a trip, visits a museum, science center, zoo, or other attraction, purchase a souvenir patch from the gift shop. Sew or use fabric adhesive to attach the patch to the blanket. The blanket will then act as a physical memorial to the memories you make through the years. Use it as an Ebenezer stone to recall and recount what God has orchestrated in your lives.

Create a neighborhood traveling basket. Fill a gently used basket with inexpensive "fun" such as a new card game, candy, tea, a joke book, and/or baked goods. Include a card of encouragement and deliver the basket to a friend or neighbor. Explain that it is a traveling basket. Encourage the recipient to enjoy the contents and then invite them to pass the basket on to another friend, refilling and replacing the items as needed. Attach a tag on the side of the basket, providing space for each future giftee to write his or her name and the date. In that way, each new person or family can see how "far" the basket has traveled to reach them.

Make blessings bags. Fill gallon-sized zipper bags with items for the homeless in your community. Keep one or two of these bags in the back of your car to distribute on your daily commute. For cost-effectiveness, purchase items in bulk and divide these among multiple bags. Bag contents could include personal hygiene items, feminine products (for women's bags), a bottle of water, prepackaged snacks, a pair of new socks, sunscreen, hand and foot warmers, a mini sewing/repair kit, public transit tokens/cards, laundromat tokens or quarters, first-aid items, a gift card to a fast-food restaurant, and a handwritten card declaring God's love.

Create a sick-day basket. When you learn that a friend or neighbor is under the weather, fill and deliver a basket with care items such as a box of tissue, throat lozenges, hot drink packs, a can of soup, a single-serve size bottle of juice, a gently used book, a book of word puzzles, or an adult coloring book.

Create a Taste-and-See basket. Fill a gently used basket with faith-forming resources for your family. Set this near the dining table. Before or after each family meal, read or recite a selection from one of the items in the basket to invite your family and guests to nourish their souls. Basket items could include a Bible or children's storybook Bible, Scripture memory cards, a missionary biography, a children's theology book such as *The Ology* by Marty Machowski (New Growth Press) or the What We Believe series by John Hay and David Webb (Apologia Press), prayer prompts, and/or a prayer journal.

Gift a traveling birthday card. Purchase a birthday card for a friend. Use it to write an encouraging note to her on the inside corner of it, and then sign and date it. Place it in the envelope, writing "Birthday Girl" on the front and the following instructions on the back: "After reading this card, store it away until my birthday. Return it with a message of encouragement for me." Do not seal the envelope. Continue to send this same card back and forth to each other every year, creating a chronology of your friendship and all that God has done in your lives.

Write a mirror message. Using a dry-erase marker on the bathroom mirror, write a message of welcome to a guest or a love note to a family member.

Create a two-person journal. Buy a spiral notebook or journal to be used to write notes to a spouse, child, or roommate. Ask the recipient meaningful questions that will help open lines of communication that might otherwise be closed. End your message with an invitation for them to use the next page in the notebook to write a letter back to you. Place the notebook in a discreet spot where only they will see it. Continue to write messages back and forth, using the pages as an opportunity to deepen the relationship. This can be an especially helpful tool when parenting during the teen years, as a confidential journal can provide a safe space for an adolescent to share struggles without the social pressure of face-to-face interaction.

Host a Little Free Lending Library. Buy or build a book box to place at the street-side edge of your yard. (You can find assembly instructions or boxes for purchase at https://littlefreelibrary.org.) Along with clean current titles, fill the box with your favorite faith-forming books, and a gently used Bible to spread the good news to those in your neighborhood. Whenever your budget allows, purchase used Bibles at thrift shops or yard sales to restock your lending library when needed. In addition, you could tell other believers you know about your book box and ask if they'd be willing to donate Bibles they are not currently using.

Write a sidewalk message. Using outdoor sidewalk chalk, write an encouraging message, a favorite Scripture passage, or a simple hopscotch-style game on your front walk for passersby to enjoy.

Host a tea exchange. Ask friends and neighbors to purchase one box or tin of their favorite tea blend. When guests arrive, add up the total number of individual tea bags/sachets that have been brought and divide that number by the number of guests in attendance. This number will determine how many bags/sachets each person will be able to select during the exchange. Place all the boxes/tins on a table or counter and invite guests to take turns selecting the bags/sachets they'd like to try. Once all the tea bags have been divided, make a pot of hot water to allow guests to sample one of their chosen brews. They may then take home the rest of their choices. Each guest may have come with several bags of one type of tea but will leave with one bag of several different types of tea, allowing them to sample a wide variety of flavors in the days to come.

Host a homespun swap. Invite friends and family to make homemade items of their choosing to bring to the swap. They may make several different items (like a jar of salsa, a handknit scarf, and a pack of hand-drawn greeting cards) or multiple versions of the same thing (like three jars of homemade pickles). When guests arrive, encourage them to barter with others to swap their homemade goods for someone else's. In this way, a neighbor who makes great salsa can share jars of it with other neighbors while receiving things like homemade bread, a bag of granola, and a crocheted dishcloth in return.

Host an old-fashioned ice cream social. Purchase a tub of vanilla and a tub of chocolate ice cream. Invite neighbors to join you for dessert, encouraging them to bring their favorite toppings to share. Set all these ingredients out with bowls and spoons to create a buffet-style serving line.

Host a S'more Taste Test. Purchase marshmallows and invite friends and neighbors to bring their favorite chocolate candy bar and/or graham-style cookie. Encourage each guest or team of guests to create a variation of the standard s'more and host a group taste test of all the choices. Encourage attendees to anonymously vote for any other s'more creation besides their own. Tally the votes and declare a winning s'more recipe.

Host a chili cook-off. Invite friends and neighbors to make a pot of chili to share. Provide bowls, spoons, and add-ins like shredded cheese, sour cream, and crackers. Place the chili pots on a counter, setting a number sign next to each pot. Scoop a few bites' worth of each chili into paper cups, marking the cups with the corresponding numbers. Provide each attendee with a spoon and one paper cup of each kind of chili. After they've sampled each variation, encourage them to vote anonymously for any other chili besides their own. Tally the votes and declare a winning recipe.

SEASONALLY SPECIFIC *HYGGE*

Curate a New Year's jar. Wash and set out a large, empty pickle jar in a prominent place in your house along with a stack of 3x5 cards and pens. Throughout the year, invite family and friends to use the cards to document their thoughts about memorable life events and place the cards in the jar. Read the cards aloud to one another on New Year's Eve. You will be creating a stack of memorial stones of God's goodness like the ones mentioned in Joshua chapter four.

Display a Resurrection Tree. Cut a small bare branch from a tree, approximately a foot or a foot-and-a-half in length. Place it in a vase and set it in a prominent place in your home. Using cardstock and ribbon, create paper ornaments of the following symbols to illustrate portions of the Easter story: a palm leaf (Matt. 21:7–9), a bag of coins (Matt. 26:14–15), a table place setting or Communion setting (Matt. 26:17–19), a length of rope (Matt. 27:1–2), a pitcher of water (Matt. 27:24–26), a crown of thorns (John 19:2), a nail (John 19:17–18), a jar of wine (John 19:28–29), a cross (Matt. 27:45–46, 50), a pair of dice (Mark 15:24), a tomb with the stone rolled in place (Mark 15:46), a tomb with the stone rolled away or a shining sun (Matt. 28:5–6). Twelve days before Easter Sunday, begin to count down to the Resurrection by encouraging a member of your family, a roommate, or a guest to hang one ornament on the tree each day and discuss its significance and/or read the corresponding Scripture out loud.

Deliver May Day baskets. Using a hole punch, make two adjacent holes at the top of a paper coffee cup. Lace/tie yarn or ribbon through the holes to make a handle. Fill the paper cup "basket" with small, edible gifts and an encouraging note. On May Day (May 1) or any day, deliver the basket to a neighbor, hanging it on their front doorknob to be discovered by them at random. Basket items could include single-serving hot cocoa packets, tea bags, individually wrapped snacks, candy, gum, seed packets, fresh-cut flowers, or a small potted plant.

Pass out gospel tracts and candy on Halloween. Purchase or make Halloween-themed gospel tracts that tell the redemptive story of salvation. (Crossway Books produces several kid-friendly Halloween tracts.) When kids come to your door asking for a trick-or-treat, give them a piece of candy along with a gospel tract.

Create a "thankfulness" tablecloth. Purchase a white or cream-colored tablecloth to cover your dining room table on Thanksgiving. In addition, buy an assortment of fabric markers in fall colors, setting them on or near the table. Invite your friends and family to use the markers to draw and write a message on the tablecloth, listing things they are most thankful for. Encourage them to sign their name and date their entries. Each year, as notes and signatures are added, the tablecloth will help you recall and recount your gratitude to God for what He has done and continues to do in the lives of those you love.

Compile a reverse Advent calendar. Starting December 1, place one non-perishable food item into a festively wrapped box each day. On Christmas Eve, deliver the box to a local food shelf or homeless shelter. In this way, you will be counting down the days until Christmas by giving an Advent treat instead of receiving one.

Create a Christmas Card Prayer Journal. Compile the Christmas cards and annual photos you receive during the holiday season in a mini photo album, fasten them together with a flashcard ring, or have them spiral bound at a local office supply shop. Use the collection as a prayer prompt at meals or during family devotions. Pick one card each day and pray for the individuals it represents.

ACKNOWLEDGMENTS

A ny words I have written about *hyggelig* living have come from the overflow of the generous *hygge* I have received from others. Like Aaron and Hur in Exodus 17, the following people have held my arms high that I might do the work of writing words.

Kristi Wikstrom, Jessica Devine, Andrea Babinski, Lauren Anderson, Jessica Fulcher, and Kaley Herman, thank you for reading every word and giving me your candid thoughts. Your feedback was indispensable and has made this a book worth reading.

Pastors Kyle Eaton and Mike Solas, you steered me straight on more than one occasion and have charged me with scriptural integrity. Thank you for holding fast to what is true and asking that I do the same.

Keely Boeving, my agent, even when all I had were a few scattered pages, you were already doing the hard work on my behalf to ensure they'd find the perfect home. Thank you for always pointing my words in the best direction.

Judy Dunagan and Annette LaPlaca, thank you for keeping watch. Your keen editorial eyes and careful consideration have shaped every page. I'm forever grateful to have had *hygge* placed in your care. Ashley Torres, Melissa Zaldivar, Erik Peterson, Kathryn Eastham, and the entire team at Moody Publishers, thank you for always listening to my input and gently guiding me with your expertise. Publishing might be the conduit, but spreading the good news of Jesus and equipping His followers is your mission—and it shows!

Kelly Hellmuth, I couldn't have asked for a more dedicated and trustworthy writing partner. Thank you for showing up day after day. Who knew that a book could be written in one hour! Tag, you're it.

Emily Gutenkauf, Jacqui Cartwright, Lora Kesselhon, Amy Johnson, Shannon Pfeffer, Jenny Roub, Liz Eaton, and Sarah Ho, Proverbs 11:14 says, "Where there is no guidance, a people falls, but in an abundance of counselors there is safety." Thank you for answering every frantic text, offering your honest thoughts, and encircling me with encouragement as I threw words at a page. Most of all, thank you for knowing me enough to "No" me whenever necessary. Your counsel kept me safe all along the way.

Maureen and Glen, yours was a home of *hygge* to me before I even knew I needed one. Thank you for always opening your door.

Mom, not a single day has passed in my life that I've not felt cocooned by your encouragement and comfort. You may not remember, but I'll never forget.

Madeline, Reese, Finnlae, Jack, and Jude, there's no one I'd rather make a home for than you. May you always look to Jesus to find your Land of Promise.

Dain, even after twenty years, it feels like we're just getting started. Our life together has been the test lab for holy *hygge*. I trust by now you know that I'd follow you anywhere, especially Minnesota.

Jesus, I pray that every word of this book whispers Your name. You are my home. You are my *hygge*.

NOTES

INTRODUCTION: MAKING HOME

Epigraph: C. S. Lewis, *Mere Christianity* (New York: HarperCollins, 1952), 136–137.

1. Louisa Thomsen Brits, *The Book of Hygge* (New York: Plume, 2017), 16.
2. Ibid, 19.
3. Meik Wiking, *The Little Book of Hygge* (New York: HarperCollins, 2017), 22–24.
4. John F. Helliwell et al., "Social Environments for World Happiness," *World Happiness Report 2020*, March 20, 2020, https://worldhappiness .report/ed/2020/social-environments-for-world-happiness/.
5. "Word of the Year 2016," OxfordLanguages, accessed January 31, 2022, https://languages.oup.com/word-of-the-year/2016/.
6. Jessica Lowry Vizzutti, "Live Your Best Hygge Life," HGTV, accessed January 31, 2022, https://www.hgtv.com/sweepstakes/hgtv-urban-oasis/2019/hgtv-urban-oasis-2019-hygge-lifestyle-pictures.
7. "#hygge," Instagram, accessed January 31, 2022, https://www.instagram .com/explore/tags/hygge/?hl=en.

8. "G3306 - menō - Strong's Greek Lexicon (KJV)," Blue Letter Bible, accessed January 31, 2022, https://www.blueletterbible.org/lexicon/g3306/kjv/tr/0-1/.

CHAPTER 1: HOSPITALITY

Epigraph: Sally Clarkson, *The Lifegiving Table* (Carol Stream, IL: Tyndale Momentum, 2017), 13.

1. "H157 - 'āhaḇ- Strong's Greek Lexicon (KJV)," Blue Letter Bible, accessed January 31, 2022, https://www.blueletterbible.org/lexicon/h157/kjv/wlc/0-1/.

2. "Jewish Practices & Rituals: Hospitality," Jewish Virtual Library, accessed January 31, 2022, https://www.jewishvirtuallibrary.org/hospitality-in-judaism.

3. Jamie Erickson (@unlikely_homeschool), "The table was important to Jesus. Or more accurately, the people around the table were important," Instagram photo, November 4, 2018, https://www.instagram.com/p/Bpx2JLgAYVe/.

4. Elena Renken, "Most Americans Are Lonely, and Our Workplace Culture May Not Be Helping," *NPR*, January 23, 2020, https://www.npr.org/sections/healthshots/2020/01/23/798676465/most-americans-are-lonely-and-our-workplace-culture-may-not-be-helping.

5. Gunnar Karl Gíslason and Jody Eddy, *The Hygge Life* (New York: Ten Speed Press, 2017), 140.

6. "Breaking Bread with 'Companion,'" Merriam-Webster, accessed February 12, 2022, https://www.merriam-webster.com/words-at-play/history-of-word-companion.

7. Roberto A. Ferdman, "The Most American Thing There Is: Eating Alone," *The Washington Post*, August 18, 2015, https://www.washingtonpost.com/news/wonk/wp/2015/08/18/eating-alone-is-a-fact-of-modern-american-life/.

8. "Had a Long Day of Travel? Check Into a Hospital," Merriam-Webster, accessed February 12, 2022, https://www.merriam-webster.com/words-at-play/word-history-hospital-hostel-hotel-hospice.

9. Jamie Erickson, "The Year of Hygge for Homeschooling," *The Unlikely Homeschool*, June 17, 2016, https://www.theunlikelyhomeschool.com/2016/06/hygge.html.

CHAPTER 2: RELATIONSHIPS

Epigraph: Fred Rogers, "What Nourishes Our Souls: Fred Rogers' Commencement Address at Marquette University," *We Are Marquette*, March 14, 2016, https://stories.marquette.edu/what-nourishes-our-souls-6ae2ba84bd26.

1. Jamie Erickson (@unlikely_homeschool), "As a mom who has heard more than her share of sibling squabbles," Instagram photo, June 11, 2020, https://www.instagram.com/p/CBT8N0lplCe/.
2. "The Health Impact of Loneliness: Emerging Evidence and Interventions," NIHCM Foundation, October 15, 2018, https://nihcm.org/publications/the-health-impact-of-loneliness-emerging-evidence-and-interventions.
3. Elena Renken, "Most Americans Are Lonely, and Our Workplace Culture May Not Be Helping," *NPR*, January 23, 2020, https://www.npr.org/sections/health-shots/2020/01/23/798676465/most-americans-are-lonely-and-our-workplace-culture-may-not-be-helping.
4. Louisa Thomsen Brits, *The Book of Hygge* (New York: Plume, 2017), 50.
5. Meik Wiking, *The Little Book of Hygge* (New York: HarperCollins, 2017), 26.
6. "Senator Benjamin E. Sasse Takes on Tribalism and Loneliness in Book," Morning Joe MSNBC, October 16, 2018, YouTube video, https://www.youtube.com/watch?v=YifkAM4nN-M&t=370s.
7. Wiking, *Little Book of Hygge*, 202.
8. Unverified quotation attributed to Theodore Roosevelt.
9. Marie Tourell Søderbergh, *Hygge: The Danish Art of Happiness* (United Kingdom: Michael Joseph, 2016), 12.
10. Annie Dillard, *The Writing Life* (New York: Harper & Row Publishers, 1989), 32.

CHAPTER 3: WELL-BEING

Epigraph: *Parade*, December 30, 1973; quoted in "Resolve to Be Tender with the Young and Compassionate with the Aged," Quote Investigator, December 22, 2014, https://quoteinvestigator.com/2014/12/22/tender/.

1. Zameena Mejia, "Harvard's Longest Study of Adult Life Reveals How You Can Be Happier and More Successful," *CNBC Make It*, March 20, 2018, https://www.cnbc.com/2018/03/20/this-harvard-study-reveals-how-you-can-be-happier-and-more-successful.html.

2. "Poverty Rate by Country 2021," World Population Review, accessed February 12, 2022, https://worldpopulationreview.com/country-rankings/poverty-rate-by-country.
3. Louisa Thomsen Brits, *The Book of Hygge* (New York: Plume, 2017), 129.
4. Beth Hautala (@rise.write.repeat), "Today was one of those Mondays that begins with lovely intention and sort of deflates," Instagram photo, November 8, 2021, https://www.instagram.com/p/CWCKNiEsp LETE0YOnRIaSMLejnmwTvjHd9SQQU0/.
5. Emily P. Freeman, "Choose Your Absence," *The Next Right Thing*, podcast audio, January 8, 2018, https://emilypfreeman.com/podcast/19/.
6. "H2165 - zᵊmān - Strong's Greek Lexicon (KJV)," Blue Letter Bible, https://www.blueletterbible.org/lexicon/h2165/kjv/wlc/0-1/.
7. Jamie Erickson (@unlikely_homeschool), "In our age of high-speed, higher-speed, highest-speed, online relationships are sometimes the hardest to care for," Instagram photo, October 20, 2020, https://www.instagram.com/p/CGkeS48hu4w/.
8. Tish Harrison Warren, *Liturgy of the Ordinary* (Downers Grove, IL: InterVarsity Press, 2016), 148.

CHAPTER 4: ATMOSPHERE

Epigraph: Winston Churchill, "Speech in the British House of Commons regarding the rebuilding of the Commons Chamber," HC Deb, October 28, 1943, vol 393 cc403–73, https://api.parliament.uk/historic-hansard/commons/1943/oct/28/house-of-commons-rebuilding.
1. "Crĕo," *Latinitium*, https://latinitium.com/latin-dictionaries/?t=lsn 11543,do117.
2. Grant Hilary Brenner, "The Secrets You Keep Are Hurting You—Here's How," *Psychology Today*, January 22, 2019, https://www.psychology today.com/us/blog/experimentations/201901/the-secrets-you-keep-are-hurting-you-heres-how.
3. Signe Johansen, *How to Hygge: The Nordic Secrets to a Happy Life* (New York: St. Martin's Press, 2017), 167.
4. Louisa Thomsen Brits, *The Book of Hygge* (New York: Plume, 2017), 98.
5. Nancy DeMoss Wolgemuth, *Lies Women Believe: And the Truth That Sets Them Free* (Chicago: Moody Publishers, 2018), 123.
6. Darby E. Saxbe and Rena Repetti, "No Place Like Home: Home Tours Correlate with Daily Patterns of Mood and Cortisol," *National Library*

of Medicine, November 23, 2009, https://pubmed.ncbi.nlm.nih.gov/ 19934011/.
7. Erma Bombeck, *Eat Less Cottage Cheese and More Ice Cream* (Kansas City, MO: Andrews McMeel Publishing, 2003).
8. Seong-Hyun Park and Richard H. Mattson, "Effects of Flowering and Foliage Plants in Hospital Rooms on Patients Recovering from Abdominal Surgery," *Hort Technology 18*, no. 4 (2008), https://doi.org/ 10.21273/HORTTECH.18.4.563.
9. "Focus," *Latinitium*, https://latinitium.com/latin-dictionaries/?t= sh10156,lsn18480.
10. Bob Smietana, "Study: Americans Fond of Bible, But How Many Read It?," *Baptist Press*, April 25, 2017, https://www.baptistpress.com/ resource-library/news/study-americans-fond-of-bible-but-how-many-read-it/.

CHAPTER 5: COMFORT

Epigraph: Rosaria Butterfield, *The Gospel Comes with a House Key* (Wheaton, IL: Crossway, 2018), 93.
1. "H1588 - *gan* - Strong's Hebrew Lexicon (KJV)," Blue Letter Bible, accessed November 15, 2021, https://www.blueletterbible.org/lexicon/ h1588/kjv/wlc/0-1/.
2. "H5731 - *'ēden* - Strong's Hebrew Lexicon (KJV)," Blue Letter Bible, accessed November 15, 2021, https://www.blueletterbible.org/lexicon/ h5731/kjv/wlc/0-1/.
3. Attributed to a Japanese proverb. See "If You Seek Revenge You Should Dig Two Graves," Quote Investigator, accessed February 14, 2022, https://quoteinvestigator.com/2019/07/07/two-graves/.
4. Louisa Thomsen Brits, *The Book of Hygge* (New York: Plume, 2017), 92.
5. Henry Cloud and John Townsend, *Boundaries* (Grand Rapids, MI: Zondervan, 1992), 94.
6. Maurus Brown and Gary Gao, "Basic Principles of Pruning Backyard Grapevines," *Ohioline: Ohio State University Extension*, February 8, 2017, https://ohioline.osu.edu/factsheet/HYG-1428.

CHAPTER 6: CONTENTMENT

Epigraph: A. A. Milne, *The House at Pooh Corner* (New York: Dell Publishing Co., 1928), 19–20.

1. Jay Friedenberg, *Artificial Psychology: The Quest for What It Means to Be Human* (New York: Taylor & Francis, 2010), 217, quoted in Greg McKeown, *Essentialism: The Disciplined Pursuit of Less* (New York: Crown Publishing Group, 2014), 26.
2. Jamie Erickson, "The Comparison Trap," *Mom to Mom Podcast*, podcast audio, April 2, 2019, http://momtomompodcast.com/4/.
3. Elisabeth Elliot, *Keep a Quiet Heart* (Ann Arbor, MI: Servant Publications, 1995), 20.
4. Richard Florida, "The Unhappy States of America," Bloomberg, March 20, 2018, https://www.bloomberg.com/news/articles/2018-03-20/gallup-study-shows-well-being-in-decline-across-america.
5. Kristen Welch, *Raising Grateful Kids in an Entitled World: How One Family Learned That Saying No Can Lead to Life's Biggest Yes* (Carol Stream, IL: Tyndale Momentum, 2015), 157.
6. Ibid., 158.
7. Hannah Ritchie and Max Roser, "Clean Water," Our World in Data, September 2019, last updated in June 2021, https://ourworldindata.org/water-access.
8. Jamie Erickson (@unlikely_homeschool), "We have a lamppost at the edge of our frontyard," Instagram, October 21, 2020, https://www.instagram.com/p/CGm9hXmBvwv/.
9. Helen Russell, *The Year of Living Danishly* (London: Icon Books, 2015), 277.

CHAPTER 7: REST

Epigraph: Bishop J. Taylor Smith, "Friends of Jesus," *The Church Missionary Review* 53 (1902), 811.
1. "H7673 - šābaṯ - Strong's Hebrew Lexicon (KJV)," Blue Letter Bible, https://www.blueletterbible.org/lexicon/h7673/kjv/wlc/0-1/.
2. Orthodox Union staff, "The 39 Categories of Sabbath Work Prohibited by Law," Orthodox Union, July 17, 2006, https://www.ou.org/holidays/the_thirty_nine_categories_of_sabbath_work_prohibited_by_law/.
3. Lydia Saad, "The '40-Hour' Workweek Is Actually Longer—by Seven Hours," *Gallup*, August 29, 2014, https://news.gallup.com/poll/175286/hour-workweek-actually-longerseven-hours.aspx.
4. Lawrence Mishel, "Vast Majority of Wage Earners Are Working Harder, and for Not Much More," Economic Policy Institute, January 30, 2013,

https://www.epi.org/publication/ib348-trends-us-work-hours-wages-1979-2007/.

5. John Pencavel, "The Productivity of Working Hours," Stanford Institute for Economic Policy Research, discussion paper no. 13-006 (October 2013), 27, https://ideas.repec.org/p/sip/dpaper/13-006.html.

6. Helen Russell, *The Year of Living Danishly* (London: Icon Books, 2015), 53.

7. Edith Schaeffer, *What Is a Family?* (Grand Rapids, MI: Baker Books, 1975), 211.

8. Keri Wyatt Kent, *Breathe: Creating Space for God in a Hectic Life* (Grand Rapids, MI: Revell, 2005), 213.

9. Sarah DiGiulio, "What Happens in Your Body and Brain While You Sleep," *NBC News*, October 9, 2017, https://www.nbcnews.com/better/health/what-happens-yourbody-brain-while-you-sleep-ncna805276.

10. "H7673 - šāḇaṯ - Strong's Greek Lexicon (HNV)," Blue Letter Bible, https://www.blueletterbible.org/lexicon/h7673/hnv/wlc/0-1/.

11. Mason King, "Entering God's Rest," The Village Church, September 2009, video, 6:36, www.tvcresources.net/resource-library/sermons/entering-gods-rest.

12. "Yoke," *Encyclopedia Britannica*, July 20, 1998, https://www.britannica.com/technology/yoke.

13. John Lawrence, *A General Treatise on Cattle, the Ox, the Sheep, and the Swine* (London: H.D. Symonds, Paternoster-Row, 1805), 229.

14. Michael Rydelnik and Michael Vanlaningham, *The Moody Bible Commentary* (Chicago: Moody Publishers, 2014), 1473.

15. J. Dwight Pentecost, "The Yoke of Jesus," *The Voice: Dallas Theological Seminary*, October 1, 2013, https://voice.dts.edu/article/the-yoke-of-jesus-j-dwight-pentecost/.

16. "H6960 - qāvâ - Strong's Greek Lexicon (KJV)," Blue Letter Bible, https://www.blueletterbible.org/lexicon/h6960/kjv/wlc/0-1/.

17. "G2218 - zygos - Strong's Greek Lexicon (KJV)," Blue Letter Bible, https://www.blueletterbible.org/lexicon/g2218/kjv/tr/0-1/.

CHAPTER 8: A HOME FOR THE HOMELESS

Epigraph: Madeleine L'Engle, *A Rock That Is Higher* (Colorado Springs: WaterBrook Press, 2001), 340.

1. Charles Dickens, *A Christmas Carol* (New York: Simon & Schuster, 1983), 59.

Quiet the voices of "not good enough" and step
courageously into guilt-free homeschooling.

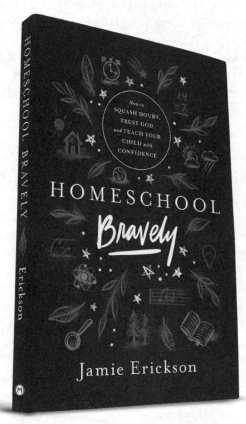

MOODY Publishers

From the Word to Life

Homeschool Bravely teaches you to see homeschooling as
a calling, helps you overthrow the tyranny of impossible
expectations, and guides you through the common bumps
in the road. Reclaim your hope, renew your purpose, and
transform your homeschool.

978-0-8024-1887-6 | also available as an eBook

The heavens are declaring.
Are you listening?

Do you feel too busy to pray? Then you're invited to find REST in God's loving presence.

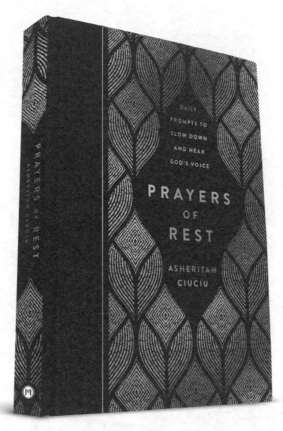

MOODY
Publishers

*From the Word **to** Life*

Asheritah Ciuciu offers you a respite from your spiritual to-do list. She provides guided prayers that will focus your mind and heart on Scripture. Using a memorable acronym and daily Bible verses, this prayer devotional will guide you through worship, confession, stillness, and surrender.

978-0-8024-1948-4 | also available as an eBook